CYPRUS BETWEEN EAST AND WEST

Studies in International Affairs Number 7

Studies in International Affairs Number 7

CYPRUS
BETWEEN
EAST AND WEST

by T. W. Adams and *Alvin J. Cottrell*

The Washington Center of Foreign Policy Research
School of Advanced International Studies
The Johns Hopkins University

The Johns Hopkins Press, Baltimore   *1968*

TO
Our daughters
Angela Adams
and
Alexandra Cottrell

FOREWORD

The persistence of some seemingly insoluble local conflicts has characterized international politics since World War II. These conflicts repeatedly disturb the relations of the major states, especially when they result or seem about to result in a local war that might expand to dangerous proportions by becoming entangled with the U.S.-Soviet competition. Paradoxically, though, a major reason for the persistence of such conflicts is that one or sometimes both of the superpowers, anxious that their involvements in local conflicts should not lead to direct confrontations with each other, try to prevent them from resulting in wars (or at least in decisive wars)—which are historically a primary means of settling such conflicts.

Cyprus is the scene of one of these persistent local conflicts. It is an especially dangerous one because of its delicate position in the East-West contest. It is a particularly complicated dispute because of the number of states, parties, and factions that are directly or indirectly involved. The authors of this study examine the pertinent events and issues and present a uniquely valuable analysis of the Cyprus conflict. In so doing they add an important chapter to the literature on contemporary international trouble spots.

This is the seventh title to be published in our Studies in International Affairs Series. The Series is designed to provide a medium-length publications format for analyses of current issues in international politics.

December 1967   ROBERT E. OSGOOD
Director
Washington Center of
Foreign Policy Research

ACKNOWLEDGMENTS

We wish to express our profound gratitude to the Relm Foundation of Ann Arbor, Michigan for a generous research grant. This grant enabled us to undertake the necessary data collection, including several field trips to the United Kingdom, Cyprus, Greece, and Turkey, to obtain first-hand knowledge of the problem as viewed by the various principals. The grant also made it possible for us to forego other commitments and to concentrate primarily upon our analysis of this complex problem.

We are deeply indebted to Anne M. Jonas, who served as a consultant to us, for her detailed comments on several drafts of the manuscript. Mrs. Jonas, a specialist on communism and the implications of Soviet politico-military policy for U.S. national security, furnished data from published Soviet sources which we added to the final version of Chapter IV. Her constructive criticism permitted us to supplement and refine our initial analysis of Soviet policy toward Cyprus, the interactions between Moscow and the Cypriot Communist Party, and the implications for U.S. policy of communist involvement in the dispute.

We also thank Dr. Robert E. Osgood, Director of the Washington Center for Foreign Policy Research, School of Advanced International Studies, The Johns Hopkins University, and Miss Naomi Schwiesow of his staff for their very useful comments.

Many other scholars and government officials—both in Western Europe and in the United States—contributed significantly to the broadening of our perspectives and furnished valuable comments on various issues. These individuals constitute too large a group to list by name.

Finally, we wish to thank the U.S. Information Agency, publishers of *Problems of Communism*, for permission to reprint portions of an earlier article by us which appeared in the May–June 1966 issue of that distinguished journal, and The Institute for Strategic Studies, London, for permission to reprint the Greek-Turkish military balance from their annual report entitled *The Military Balance, 1967–1968*.

We alone, of course, are responsible for the information presented and the conclusions drawn.

Washington, D.C.   T. W. ADAMS
December 1967   ALVIN J. COTTRELL

CONTENTS

		Page
I.	Introduction	3
II.	The Roots of the Contemporary Problem	6
III.	Communism in Cyprus	14
IV.	Soviet Policy toward Cyprus	29
V.	U.S. Policy toward Cyprus	55
VI.	The Outlook	76
Chronology		80
Greek-Turkish Military Balance (1967)		84
Selected Readings		87
Notes		88

CYPRUS BETWEEN EAST AND WEST

Studies in International Affairs Number 7

I. INTRODUCTION

In today's interlocked world, an old dictum about man can be applied to nation-states as well: Politically speaking, no country is an island unto itself—even when it happens to be an island. The convulsive events that in past times transpired virtually unnoticed in remote corners of the earth today almost instantly send tremors through the international environment. The kinds of conflicts that in other eras could be easily stamped out and left to spend themselves in isolation today flare uncomfortably close to the delayed fuses of greater conflagration. This change in the politico-military concern of the great powers with small trouble spots has created a central and bedeviling perplexity for American foreign policy, one which asserts itself almost every time tensions threaten to erupt into armed struggle. Invariably, the policy problem for the United States is translated into the task of walking a precarious tightrope between the risks of passivity and the dangers of intervention.

This diplomatic predicament has been starkly illustrated in the case of Cyprus. Ever since the internecine outburst engulfed that unhappy island in December 1963, the United States has given high-level attention as well as financial resources in efforts to solve a problem that, by the analogous standards of a metropolitan environment, could be classed as a "neighborhood rumble." The direct stakes involved for the United States in this Mediterranean island—which is half the size of New Jersey with fewer inhabitants than Denver—are a negligible part of the global sweep of American power and vital interests. This "neighborhood rumble," occurring on a piece of land remote from the great concentrations of modern demographic and industrial power, has wider implications for a strategically significant sector of the West's defenses. Moreover, it has also confounded America's alliance policy. Cyprus illuminates not only the challenges of peace-making and peace-keeping in the mid-twentieth century, but also the complex and precarious terrain upon which U.S. diplomacy must function.

In 1964, Under Secretary of State George W. Ball listed the reasons for the American concern over Cyprus:

First, as a result of ethnic ties and a complicated treaty structure, this local quarrel threatens to produce an armed conflict between Greece and Turkey.

Second, it affects the relations of the Greek and Turkish governments with the government of Cyprus.

Third, it concerns Great Britain as one of the guarantor powers with strategic bases on the Island.

Fourth, it involves the relationship of the Government of Cyprus to the British Commonwealth, of which it is a member.

Fifth, it threatens the stability of one flank of our NATO defenses and consequently concerns all NATO partners.

Sixth, because the U.N. Security Council has undertaken to keep peace on the Island, the Cyprus problem has become an active item in the [international] parliamentary diplomacy practiced in New York.

Seventh, it has stimulated a new relationship between the Government of Cyprus and other non-aligned countries with which it has recently sought to associate itself. And,

Eighth, because of Archbishop Makarios' flirtations with Moscow [and the strength of the legal indigenous Communist Party (AKEL)] this local quarrel could bring about the intrusion of the Soviet Union into the strategic Eastern Mediterranean.[1]

All of these factors are interconnected. Dwelling on only one element of the problem at a time therefore usually frustrates the effectiveness of those specialists who are searching for an over-all solution.

Politically, little has changed in the situation since 1964. The flare-up in November 1967 can be viewed as another episode in a succession of crises that have demanded intensive and protracted diplomacy to avert a war of sweeping proportions.

Thus far the turbulent and chronic feud on the island has been reasonably contained and quarantined by the combined efforts of many nations, including the operation of the highly successful United Nations peace-keeping force (UNFICYP). But a durable solution has yet to be forged. In the case of Cyprus, as in most of the complex international crises of our time, much of the relevant day-to-day U.S. diplomacy is absorbed by the constant effort to widen the community of the concerned, to spread the risks, and to share the burdens of finding a lasting peace.

II. THE ROOTS OF THE CONTEMPORARY PROBLEM

The Cyprus problem today is basically one of communal frustrations arising from the attempts of the majority Greek and the minority Turkish communities to live together on an island where the rights and privileges of both are rigidly defined by the terms under which independence was granted. To complicate matters further, Cyprus is next door to Turkey and not far from Greece. For understandable reasons, the Cyprus problem, for both Greece and Turkey, involves chauvinism and ethnic pride. The inner circle of disputants thus includes the Cypriots, the mainland Greeks, the Turks, and also the British. The outer perimeter encompasses the U.S., the U.S.S.R., the U.A.R., NATO, and the United Nations.

The 1959 Zurich-London agreements and the resultant Cypriot constitution brought a temporary end to five years of violence on the island, and were intended to provide a formula whereby the Greek and Turkish Cypriot communities could live together in peace. The shortcoming of the agreements was that they embodied a compromise solution initially worked out by Greece, Turkey, and Great Britain and presented to the Cypriot people as a Hobson's choice. The solution was at best a *détente*, and was clearly no victory for any of the contenders. The crux of the problem in Cyprus seems upon superficial examination to be the failure of the Zurich-London agreements to operate to the satisfaction of all the parties concerned. But when one examines the problem in greater depth, it is clear that these agreements, which were attempts to satisfy the conflicting demands of all parties to the negotiations, have not provided a flexible enough framework to meet changing conditions. The historic roots of earlier unrest could not and did not disappear with the ratification of the agreements, the achievement of independence for the island, or the subsequent efforts of the Cypriot government.

The compromise effected at Zurich and London created an independent Cyprus, protected by the United Kingdom, Greece, and Turkey under a Treaty of Guarantee. The British, who initially wanted to retain full sovereignty, ended by keeping only their bases. The Greeks and the Greek Cypriots had wanted *enosis* (union with Greece), but instead got an independent political entity. The Turks and the Turkish Cypriots had wanted to keep the British presence as a buffer between the two ethnic communities and, when this seemed impossible, their policy became that of *taksim* (partition of the island). In the end, Turkey, along with Greece, acquired the right of military intervention, if this should become necessary to protect the interests of their respective "blood brothers" on the island. The Turkish Cypriots also received very extensive guarantees that their interests would be safeguarded—more extensive, perhaps, than any ever written into a constitution for the protection of a minority community.

The island's history, too, complicates the present-day attempts of the Cypriots to live together peacefully. For example, the Greeks, who date their presence on the island back to earliest recorded history, have traditionally viewed Cyprus as a natural part of the greater Hellenic community. Prior to 1950 this attachment represented, particularly among the Greek Cypriot villagers, an emotional and sentimental bond of kinship. The idea of *enosis* symbolized for them more of a cultural than a political union, and on this basis it could elicit a high degree of emotional reaction. In addition, many observers have characterized the Greeks as an extremely democratic and individualistic people, likely to resent regimentation and governance by a strong impersonal authority of the type which was prevalent during Cyprus's long history of foreign rule.

Long before Cyprus became independent, whoever stood in the way of *enosis* was considered by the Greek Cypriots to be the enemy. When Greece fought for her independence in the 1820s, leaving Cyprus under occupation, the enemies were the Ottoman Turks. But after 1878, when the Ottoman sultan ceded the island to Great Britain, the British became the enemy. Animosity toward the British may partially account for the development of a measure of temporary concord between the Greeks and Turks on the island. It is important to note that the harmony which the two communities experienced, especially throughout World War II, vanished only during the latter part of the 1955–59 Emergency Period in Cyprus, when the British resorted to a "divide and rule" policy.

After the postwar wave of independence swept through the British colonies and the church-run plebiscite in Cyprus in 1950 gave *enosis* a 96 percent affirmative vote by Greek Cypriots, a fiercely nationalistic movement was regenerated. In reaction to this greater emphasis on *enosis*, portending that Cyprus might actually become a political entity of Greece, the Turkish Cypriots became more "Turkish" than they had been in centuries. The Turks, maintaining the proud attitude of the *ghazi* conquerors, who ruled Cyprus for three hundred years, feared that they might become a minority,

politically controlled by former subjects of the Ottoman Empire.

At first the object of Greek resentment was the British
administration and its refusal to allow self-determination for the Cypriots. The Greeks were joined in this
opposition by some of the Turks, and anti-British forces
began pitting themselves against pro-British elements
in Cyprus. In the mid-1950s, therefore, the Greek Cypriot community was not necessarily fighting the Turkish
Cypriot community. It was true, however, that Turkish
Cypriot government officials, either to frustrate those
policies of the Greek Cypriots which could have made
them subjects of Greece, or merely because they were
conditioned to accept authority, unanimously supported
the British administrators. The Greeks, increasingly re-
sentful of British administration, were irritated both by
Turkish Cypriot support of the British and by the fact
that this Turkish-British alliance frequently thwarted
Greek policies. By 1959, most Turkish Cypriots were
looked upon as collaborators with the British against
the militant Greek Cypriot drive for self-determination.
The situation thus evolved into one of island Greeks
versus island Turks. Latent attitudes and dormant irritations came to the fore, magnified by the nationalistic
identification of both communities with their respective
fatherlands.

As long as Cyprus was under Ottoman or British control, the Turkish Cypriots were not concerned about
their minority relationship with the Greek Cypriots.
In fact, concerted anti-*enosis* violence on the part of the
Turkish Cypriots emerged only after 1958, when the
Turks evidently realized that they would have to take
measures against the day when they might find themselves without British protection. When the British decided to withdraw, the Turks became extremely wor-

ried about their security on the self-governing island and demanded the extensive guarantees provided in the Zurich-London agreements. Although these guarantees were acceptable in 1959 the Greek-Cypriots now feel that the guarantees have become privileges by which the minority can thwart the rule of the majority.

After August 1960, it quickly became clear that the Republic of Cyprus's limited form of independence had not solved many of the problems long extant between her two ethnic communities. In some instances independence had even magnified old quarrels. On the island, the Greek president and the Turkish vice-president, along with the ethnically divided House of Representatives, could not agree on such problems as the formulation of an army, the division of civil service jobs between Greeks and Turks on a 70:30 ratio, the establishment of a personal income tax system, and the question of joint versus separate administration of the Republic's five main municipalities. The operation of the central government during its first three years of existence resulted in a stalemate, and attempts by the constitutionally established courts to litigate the issues were not honored.

Problems not solved by the democratic process were soon left to other means of resolution—murder, bombings, and intimidation. The tense atmosphere elicited unyielding positions from both ethnic communities. The nationalistic agitation of the Greek Cypriots for sweeping amendments to the constitution and for the abrogation of the Zurich-London agreements (*rebus sic stantibus*) met with an adamant avowal by the Turkish Cypriots to uphold the agreements to the letter (*pacta sund servanda*). Throughout the political controversy which followed the acquisition of limited independence, both sides obtained arms—allegedly to defend themselves against the other side, if and when an attack occurred.

The pitched battles between Greek and Turkish Cypriots that began in late 1963 were an inevitable consequence of the day-to-day irritations, the historic animosities, and the extreme nationalism of the two communities. This was not a spontaneous or relatively unprovoked flare-up. It had been in the making—in part consciously, in part uncontrollably—for years. The emotions of a majority of the islanders were probably fanned into a fierce, nationalistic reaction by a relatively small number of people, some of them Cypriots and some foreign *agents provocateurs* and opportunistic interlopers. It appears plausible that the majority of the native Cypriots, had they been left alone, would still be coexisting in peace. Unfortunately, the Greek and Turkish communities harbored a latent distrust of one another which could be, and was, exploited to create overt hostility.

The salient characteristic of present-day politics in Cyprus is the absolute breakdown of Greek and Turkish intercommunal relations. Self-government within the limits of the Zurich-London agreements now is looked upon as a temporary arrangement by the Greek Cypriots, who reject any of the special minority rights for the Turkish community called for in the 1959 constitution. Instead, the Greek majority advocates a unitary state which could gain for them full political control of the island. By contrast, the Turkish Cypriots want some sort of federation, which they claim could be worked out under the existing Cyprus treaties. Obvious differences between the two indigenous communities over what they envisage as the most propitious solution to the present ineffective political arrangement still affect, and are affected by, both the foreign relations between Greece and Turkey and the extent to which these two nations support their respective Cypriot communities. Greece and Turkey, though allies since the 1934 Balkan Pact and now allies in NATO, cannot help but be deeply involved in developments in Cyprus, by virtue of their special treaty roles as guarantors of Cyprus's independence and by their natural identification with their ethnic counterparts. The foreign policy options open to the U.S. under such conditions are as narrow as the proverbial tightrope.

The faction which seems to have benefited most from the "incoherent war" which has persisted since 1963 in Cyprus is the indigenous communist party, AKEL.[2] Political parties, with the exception of the communists, are loosely organized and offer no effective deterrent to the growth of AKEL. Even the strongest labor union, the Pan-Cyprian Federation of Labor (PEO), is communist-dominated. Most Greek Cypriots at first saw no threat in AKEL's support of their national leader, Makarios, but now some of them recognize that such support was a tactic and that the communist threat is real.

Today, the Greek and Turkish Cypriots are so engrossed in battling one another that the issues of communism per se and the threat of an attempt by AKEL to seize power have been pushed into the background, at least temporarily. The political and strategic aims of the Kremlin in regard to the Eastern Mediterranean have been clearly revealed by Soviet pronouncements and actions. Cuba has provided the Soviet leaders with one example of the revolutionary opportunities available when outposts espousing the communist cause can be established in politically sensitive regions affecting the larger East-West military balance. The Soviet Union has always opposed *enosis*, though it has given lip-service to self-determination. Russia sees a much greater possibility of communism's gradually gaining additional strength and influence in an independent Cyprus than in a Cyprus which is a part of Greece. Moscow, therefore, is now insisting that the Cypriots be left alone to work out for themselves a settlement of the internal conflict, an approach that could very well dissolve the Zurich-London agreements, jeopardize the British bases in Cyprus, further divide NATO, and cause a war between Greece and Turkey.

Although Greece, Turkey, and Great Britain might prefer to detach themselves from internal Cypriot affairs, the national interests of each of these countries prevent so simple a course of action. The Greek Cypriot government insists that it has a voice equal to any of the principal parties in all decisions which affect the foreign or domestic affairs of the Republic. The Makarios government believes it is fighting a straightforward battle for the universally accepted principle of self-determination. Greek Cypriots think they are capable of solving their own problems without the intervention of foreign powers. Nevertheless, as long as Greece, Turkey, or any of the major powers find reason to disagree with the Greek Cypriot view, instability on Cyprus will not be solely a domestic matter.

Although there is considerable difference of opinion regarding the size and effectiveness of AKEL, it is generally conceded to be the only well-organized political force that could rival the dominant, though amorphous, grouping of church-backed, right-wing factions known as the Patriotic Front—the personal party of Archbishop-President Makarios III.

AKEL maintains a cohesive grass roots base and is cleverly managed by a shrewd and fervent long-time Marxist, Ezekias Papaioannou. As far as is known, AKEL is entirely Greek Cypriot in composition and numbers approximately 10,000 members, or about 3 percent of the island's adult population. Its support comes from a leftist labor federation of about 40,000 members and from a series of front organizations for farmers, women, and youth. Whether or not the party could control a third of the electorate if new elections were held, as has been claimed by AKEL's leaders, would depend upon the political issues which emerged as most vital during a pre-election campaign. Nevertheless, it is clear that, on a percentage-of-population basis, the Communist Party of Cyprus is numerically one of the strongest in the noncommunist world, second only to that of Italy.

The Rise of the Party

Communism first came to Cyprus in 1926. AKEL's predecessor, the KKK (Kommonistikon Komma Kyprou—the Communist Party of Cyprus), was recognized by the Comintern in 1928. But it did not have enough appeal to combat the power of the Orthodox Church over the predominantly agrarian and religiously oriented society of that time. The KKK was officially banned by the British colonial government in 1933 after island-wide riots involving the party.

AKEL was formally founded in 1941 and at first was far from being hard-core communist. It began as a left-wing debating society that initially attracted many liberal intellectuals but the communists were to gain control openly in less than two years. Toward the end of World War II, the reorganized party gained considerable ground through the efforts of a number of Greek Cypriot high school teachers, combined with its tactical support of *enosis*, although most of the intellectuals left as the communists took over. AKEL had become the strongest political organization in Cyprus by 1946, when it won the local elections in five major cities.

The Greek Orthodox Church soon recognized AKEL's growing power and the danger it implied. When Makarios II was elected Archbishop in 1947, he encouraged the formation of another political party catering to the right-wing middle class. (From the beginning of the Ethnarchy idea under the Ottomans, the backing of the Church had usually been the key to success in Cypriot politics.) This new Church-backed party, the Nationalist Party, quite naturally made *enosis* its main political platform, but was still a rather loosely organized moral front. In the municipal elections of 1949, the right-wing *enosists* gained 60 percent of the popular vote, winning back the capital, Nicosia, and eleven of fifteen municipalities, while AKEL maintained its control of the large port cities of Limassol, Famagusta, and Larnaca. By the time the so-called Emergency

Period was proclaimed six years later, the charismatic Makarios III—subsequently to become president of the Republic—was thought to have reduced AKEL's following from nearly 40 percent of the population to 20 percent.

AKEL and Grivas

During the Emergency Period (1955–59), when it was proscribed by the British for subversive activities, AKEL continued to conduct an active undercover campaign for unconditional self-determination for Cyprus. By this time the party had discontinued its overt support for *enosis*, which caused it to lose favor with the Greek Cypriot followers of General George Grivas (Dighenis) and his EOKA[3] guerrilla organization, then engaged in struggle against the British. Although Grivas made it clear that he would not accept AKEL's support, the party has never been able to live down the memory of its opposition to the EOKA campaign. In the words of Grivas: "In opposing us, the Cypriot Communists were simply taking orders from behind the Iron Curtain; this was clearly shown in the first month of our campaign, when in a broadcast from Moscow, the leader of the Greek Communist Party, Zachariades, denounced EOKA and treacherously revealed the identity of Dighenis, which he had learned from one of his Athenian spies."[4]

Greek Cypriots not only condemned the communists for playing a negative role during the EOKA struggle, but accused them of active collaboration with the British colonial government. This opinion did not change even though party Secretary General Papaioannou was arrested, along with fifty-eight other leftists, by the colonial government in 1955. Papaioannou escaped the following year and paradoxically turned up in Britain in 1957. He returned to Nicosia a year later and took over the party before the ban was lifted on its activities in 1959, just before independence.

AKEL is guided by revolutionary motives which, in the final analysis, are unconnected with Cypriot national interests. The party takes its directions primarily from Russia. In retrospect, the failure of the communists to participate in the EOKA movement was a tactical if not a strategic mistake. As in similar movements elsewhere, the right-wing character of the EOKA struggle should not have ideologically inhibited the communists from participating in the fight for national independence. Their withdrawal from the EOKA struggle lost them indigenous support and made them appear to be allies of the British "imperialists." The Cypriot Communist Party probably erred in not cooperating with EOKA in 1955 in part because of criticism for what the Comintern deemed as their unsatisfactory role in a 1931 anti-British uprising. By the end of the EOKA period, the position of the communists in the Greek Cypriot community had further deteriorated and dissension emerged in the AKEL ranks.

There is much evidence that AKEL worked closely with Moscow just before and after independence. Cypriot communists made frequent trips to the U.S.S.R. Soviet propaganda was broadcast in Greek to Cyprus daily from Radio Budapest, and the Cypriot communists began to identify themselves with the Castro revolution in Cuba. In October 1960 Papaioannou attended the 43rd anniversary of the Soviet Revolution in Moscow and stayed for the conference of eighty-one communist parties the following month. An editorial in the Cypriot communist paper *Haravghi* (*Dawn*) in December praised the Moscow conference's declaration, hailing the Communist Party of Russia as the "vanguard of the Communist movement." The declaration, said the paper, "constitutes a sermon and motive of brotherly struggle for peace all over the world."[5]

Since independence, AKEL has denounced the Zurich-London agreements of 1959 as a complete renunciation of the principles of self-determination. In particular, it has complained that the British Sovereign Base Areas guaranteed by the agreements constitute neo-colonialism. AKEL's central committee defined its position as follows: "Under the regime imposed by the Zurich-London agreements, and since we are far from having gained true independence, the basic goal of the Cyprian people continues to be real independence for Cyprus, demilitarization of Cyprus, and democratization of the constitution."[6]

Over the past six years AKEL has tried to give the party a patriotic image in domestic affairs in order to allay the memory of its failure to support General Grivas against the British and its equivocal position on *enosis*. Also, by patiently supporting the government, the Cypriot communists avoided persecution or proscription. Party leaders have concentrated on improving AKEL's internal efficiency and on extending their influence among workers and young people. AKEL's present economic platform is believed to follow the party's basic program, drafted in 1959 and revised in 1962, which called for intensive agricultural development and extensive land reform through "confiscation and distribution of large private, church, and government lands among the impoverished peasants."[7]

Sources of Power

Through a combination of the formal party apparatus and its front groups and other semi-clandestine elements, AKEL continues to extend its influence into workshops, villages, farms, and certain businesses in Cyprus. The principal source of AKEL's power is the Pan-Cyprian Federation of Labor (Pankypria Ergatiki Omospondia—PEO). The PEO is affiliated with the communist-led World Federation of Trade Unions (WFTU). Its Secretary General, Andreas Ziartides, is a very able and shrewd communist, a member of the WFTU Executive Committee, and a member of the Central Committee of AKEL. Ziartides says he is a self-taught Marxist.

With an estimated dues-paying membership (as of November 1963) of 37,400 workers, the PEO embraces about 60 percent of organized labor on the island. (Of the 130,000 wage earners in Cyprus, less than 50 percent are organized.) Its nearest rival, the right-wing Confederation of Cypriot Workers (Synomospondia Ergaton Kyprou—SEK), has about 17,830 members[8] and is less efficiently run. Many workers probably belong to the PEO simply because it is the most effective labor union in Cyprus and has the ability to win superior benefits, rather than because of its communist affiliations. PEO is the main supporter of the government's wage and economic development policies.

The PEO supports AKEL's main propaganda lines, such as the demand for Cypriot self-determination, opposition to NATO, and the adoption of a nuclear-free zone in the Mediterranean. Before the outbreak of violence in 1963, PEO declared its support of President Makarios on the issue of an appeal to the United Nations to resist foreign intervention in Cypriot affairs. In mid-1965 PEO repeated its pledge of unqualified support for the President's bid to revise the Zurich-London agreements and the constitution.

The sporadic efforts of the Makarios government— sometimes stimulated by Greece and even the U.S., as well as by General Grivas—to break the communists' grip on the labor movement has proved to be a difficult task. The PEO is firmly entrenched, having become well developed before Cyprus gained independence. Its leadership is vastly better trained and better paid (including gratuities such as cars, medical care, scholarships, and vacations in Eastern Europe) than that of the noncommunist SEK. Furthermore, the wives and children of PEO members constitute the majority of the memberships of AKEL's women's group and youth movement.

Strategy and Tactics

AKEL's slogans have rarely changed since independence in 1960. The scene at the party's 11th Congress held at Nicosia in March 1966 was described in these terms: "The big hall in which the Congress is meeting is bedecked with slogans and posters calling upon the people of Cyprus to rally in a united anti-imperialist front to struggle for the complete national independence of Cyprus, for the ending of foreign military bases on the island, and for the vital and democratic rights of the people."[9]

Since the establishment of the Republic, despite occasional policy differences with Moscow, AKEL's propaganda line has consistently credited "the existence of the Soviet Union and the socialist camp" with providing the kind of system "for building a truly independent economic and political life in Cyprus, free of any economic and political bondage imposed on us by the imperialists-colonialists."[10] In terms of current Soviet theory and practice regarding the achievement of "national democracy" as the precursor of socialist "people's democracy," AKEL is still in the first stage of communist revolutionary campaigning—that of "national democratic," "anti-imperialist," and "national liberation" struggle.

AKEL has used its political power to urge that Cyprus accept offers of barter agreements, economic aid, and technical assistance from the communist-ruled countries. The island's communist newspaper, *Haravghi*, has also supported the Soviet tactical line of attacking the presence of British bases and American communications facilities on the island, claiming that it is the West's intention to turn Cyprus into a nuclear base. Editorial statements in *Haravghi* depict the Soviet Union as the sole leader in the cause of world peace: "It is enough for the peoples to be mobilized in time and not to allow the warmongering imperialists to trap the popular masses in their nets. The general and complete destruction of all nuclear weapons of massive destruction, for which the people are fighting under the leadership of the Soviet Union, constitutes the only real guarantee for peace."[11]

It should be noted here that the Cypriot communists have explicitly aligned themselves with the Soviet Union in the Sino-Soviet split. On September 29, 1963, following a plenary session, the party central committee issued a 5,000-word statement which included a passage denouncing the Chinese communists and their "civil war methodology." The statement declared that AKEL's aim was to bring about a communist Cyprus, but that the "proper" way to achieve this was through "absolutely democratic and peaceful methods."[12] Secretary General Papaioannou reconfirmed the party's position in 1966 at AKEL's 11th Congress, stating that "our party condemns all splitting activities and fully supports the striving of the CPSU and other fraternal parties for the firm unity of the international Communist and workers' movement."[13]

Although AKEL publicly espoused the cause of self-determination and demilitarization, it has not clarified its position on *enosis*, and it is on this issue that the greatest strain has developed between the party and the Greek Cypriot community. (The party also differs with Moscow on this question—see Chapter IV.) AKEL leaders realize that publicly they must pay lip service to *enosis* lest the party lose much of its popular support. Thus, PEO and AKEL leader Andreas Ziartides told one of the authors: "What we want is national liberation, and in Cyprus this means *enosis*—but we want genuine *enosis*, not the kind proposed by the imperialists as in the recommendations of Dean Acheson."[14] On the other hand, the AKEL leadership is aware that, should *enosis* come about, the party would lose its legal status under a mainland Greek government. (Communism has been banned in Greece since 1949.) Apparently, however, AKEL feels safe in straddling the fence on this issue, optimistically sensing that the possibility of union with Greece is becoming increasingly remote.

The party has come out in favor of the Makarios government's view that, so long as "genuine and untrammeled" *enosis* is not obtainable, the only right course is to proceed toward unrestricted independence through recommendations made in the March 1965 report of former United Nations mediator Galo Plaza of Ecuador, which ruled out both the Greek and the Turkish extreme positions and proposed a system of equal rights. The moderate *Cyprus Mail* was quick to point out that "*Haravghi*, while siding with the rest of the newspapers in welcoming the policy of support for the Plaza report, toes the communist line by demanding that the government go beyond that and call for the abolition of [all foreign military] bases."[15]

The current position of AKEL, which is lip service to *enosis* and tactical criticism of the Soviet Union's policy toward Cyprus, should be viewed in the light of the party's past record of seemingly apostate policy changes. If its tactic of supporting the national government of President Makarios becomes unpalatable, it can quickly and easily switch to the opposition. If the interests of international communism should call for it, a program of strikes, riots, arson, and intimidation could be initiated—as in 1948 when protracted violence was used in an unsuccessful attempt to dislodge the new right-wing union. The result could damage the economy, undermine the Makarios government's position, and cause a wider opening to the Left.

AKEL and the Archbishop

If it is true that the Makarios government has purposely been seeking excuses to kill or by-pass *enosis*, as has been alleged by the island's right-wing press, then AKEL's indifference to the issue conveniently and logically fits in with its present conditional support of the Archbishop. To most Greek Cypriots, however, self-determination, which the communists preach with ostensible enthusiasm, and *enosis*, which they privately dislike, are one and the same thing. AKEL, of course, does not bother to explain in public its distinction between the two ideas.

Although AKEL opposed Makarios in the 1959 presidential elections, the party in 1960 concluded a mutually expedient truce with the forces of the Archbishop-President: in return for backing Makarios, the party received five seats in parliament. Since then its political strategy has been to avoid open conflict with the President. The party's official line toward him was stated soon after independence: "We support the Archbishop and President of the Republic of Cyprus on every particular issue against the colonialists and on behalf of the defense of the people's interest. We criticize him on every particular issue where his position clashes with the popular national interests."[16]

The communists have supported the President on such major issues as constitutional revision and a non-aligned foreign policy. They also have encouraged his cordial relations with Tito and Nasser and have successfully urged him to support the communist-dominated Afro-Asian Peoples' Solidarity Organization (AAPSO), whose 1963 Executive Committee met in Nicosia. It was at this meeting that Makarios reaffirmed his intention to reject all military alliances. In February, the 1967 AAPSO Conference met in Cyprus under the leadership of Dr. Vassos Lysarrides, member of parliament, and again parroted the communist line on Cyprus.

On occasion, AKEL has conducted intense campaigns for new election laws establishing proportional representation. Asserting that they polled a much higher percentage of votes in the 1960 elections to the House of Representatives than is indicated by their present representation, the Cypriot communists still received only the five seats agreed upon before the single-list balloting took place. Furthermore, AKEL points out that it was awarded only three of the twenty-six seats in the Greek Communal Chamber. Although Makarios has resisted AKEL's past demands for more representation, the increasing strength of the communists could put the Archbishop under severe strain designed to force concessions from him. AKEL certainly intends to use its appeal as a leading proponent of the Cyprus cause to further its own interests whenever elections or other opportunities arise.

The Communist Party of Cyprus also continues to deplore expenditures for a national army, but insists that once "genuine democratic parliamentary institutions are realized, they must be defended against foreign intervention."[17] AKEL's paradoxical position on this issue reflected its hostility to General Grivas, who had followed a policy of dispersing communist-indoctrinated youths among different units in the Greek Cypriot National Guard and of keeping them under scrutiny by security elements.

Makarios has allowed AKEL to operate openly. Although he has occasionally come out against the party in public pronouncements, he has taken few effective steps to structure his own Patriotic Front as a political counterforce. Ever since the EOKA period, Makarios has had his own personal differences with the fiercely anticommunist General Grivas—a fact which AKEL can only view with satisfaction. The Archbishop evidently assumes that he can control the communists and the majority of their sympathizers through the Church. It is also possible that he needs AKEL to play off against any opposition that might arise within his own political following. Moreover, the card-carrying communists are all Greeks, and in Makarios' eyes the Turks are the enemy.

With AKEL's strength remaining intact, if not actually growing, the price the Archbishop may have to pay for communist cooperation in any future election could be much higher than it was in 1960. If he should seek another pact with AKEL regarding the second national elections, it might suit the party's long-range plans to bide its time and continue building up its organization with a view to making a bid for power, or at least putting up a major contest at the polls. Unless an increased awareness of the potential threat of AKEL to his own regime develops among Makarios and his noncommunist supporters, it is quite possible that the new pronationalist image fashioned by AKEL might one day pay off, bringing realization of the party's long-range objective of increased participation in the government of Cyprus and, ultimately, full political control. To what extent these long-term goals could be realized will depend, in large measure, on the extent of future interactions and coordination of policy tactics between AKEL and the Kremlin. Recent Soviet policy toward Cyprus has done little to help AKEL improve its position for an eventual seizure of power.

The Future of Cypriot Communism

In the face of a number of reversals and embarrassments by the Soviet Union, AKEL now must work hard to maintain its influence in Cypriot domestic affairs. The communists under Papaioannou's leadership are still the "loyal opposition of His Beatitude."[18] But if economic conditions in Cyprus continue to improve, the party may be unable to exploit the issues of unemployment and unequal distribution of personal income as successfully as it has in the past. At the same time, the communists' program of land reform seems unlikely to bring any remarkable results, since the Church is the largest landholder on Cyprus. Archbishop Makarios is sensitive about the land issue and has made widespread efforts to sell Church property at reasonable prices to small farmers. The revenue from such transactions is being invested

in local or foreign businesses, which makes the Orthodox Church the wealthiest private institution in Cyprus.
Unless AKEL chooses to meet Makarios head-on in the
next elections (whenever they are held), it seems im-
probable that domestic issues such as land reform will
play an important role in the party's maneuvering in
the immediate future.

When new national elections take place, a crucial period in Cypriot internal politics can be expected. In July
1965, the Greek Cypriot-controlled House of Representatives passed a law providing that all Cypriots—
Greeks and Turks and less significant minorities—vote
for candidates on a single electoral list, rather than on
separate lists for the Greek and Turkish communities as
the Republic's constitution originally specified. The effect of this might be to enable AKEL, by appealing to
Greek Cypriot nationalism, to make significant gains in
its share of seats in the House of Representatives. With
its strong labor and front-group support, the party also
could have a good chance of winning local control of
the five major urban areas if municipal as well as national elections were to be held in the near future.

If, on the other hand, AKEL should fail to gain its
objectives through democratic means, or be outlawed as
a result of pressure from the Grivas faction, it will still
have the less plausible option of attempting a coup
d'état at an opportune period in the future. The party
possesses three vital prerequisites for such a course—a
tightly-knit conspiratorial organization, the support of
a considerable segment of the population, and, despite
certain policy differences with the Kremlin, aid from
Russia and her allies.

Events to date seem to indicate that most noncommunist Greek Cypriots do not regard communism as a major threat to the achievement of their own long-range

political objectives. The Turks initially drew attention to the communist danger in Cyprus primarily because AKEL is composed of Greek Cypriots. The mainland Greeks, on the other hand, have tended to belittle the threat. The right-wing military junta, however, surely has definite plans on what to do about the growth of Cypriot communism even if *enosis* should never occur. One can only speculate as to what these plans entail. Under such circumstances, the future course of Cypriot communism is not clearly discernible. The party leaders have shown themselves to be patient men, and they have lived through adversities and threats more serious than any they now face.

POSTSCRIPT: A presidential election was held in Cyprus on February 25, 1968. President Makarios received 95 percent of the Greek Cypriot vote running against a fervent advocate of *enosis*. This result indicates that Makarios still commands overwhelming support of the Greek population of Cyprus even though he now appears to favor continued independence of the island.

IV. SOVIET POLICY TOWARD CYPRUS

The Soviet Union has attempted to exploit the unrest on Cyprus throughout the post-World War II era. In so doing, the U.S.S.R. has had to consider the impact of its position on the Cypriot communists, the Greek majority on the island led by Archbishop Makarios, the Turkish minority, and on Greece, Turkey, the United Kingdom, and the United States. To a lesser extent, the Soviet position toward Cyprus has at various times affected the U.S.S.R.'s relations with all NATO states and with the United Nations. Soviet policy also has had to take into account the vehement anticommunist stance of General Grivas, founder of EOKA and from 1960 to mid-November 1967 commander of the Greek Cypriot National Guard.

Under the circumstances, it is not surprising that Soviet policy toward Cyprus since the early 1950s has sometimes appeared ambivalent and contradictory. However, in the final analysis, the Soviet leaders' fundamental *strategic* objectives vis-à-vis Cyprus have remained constant. Despite continual shifts in tactics, they have consistently sought to:

(a) Exploit the dissension connected with the Cyprus issue in order to supplement other moves in their long-range campaign to intensify divisions within the NATO alliance;

(b) Insure the removal of all vestiges of British influence on the island, including the abrogation of U.K. military base and overflight rights; and

(c) Keep alive the unrest and political instability in Cyprus, thereby at least partially diverting the attention of the leaders of the U.S., the U.K., Greece, and Turkey from other problems.

During 1967, there was a significant increase in Soviet naval operations in the Mediterranean. In addition, for the first time, the overt portion of the U.S.S.R.'s annual military budget for 1968 included an allocation of funds for arms shipments and other military assistance to third world nations and national liberation movements. Hence, the strategic significance of the Cyprus problem had, by Autumn 1967, begun to increase. Its relationship to other issues affecting the East-West political-military balance had become more intense.

Soviet tactics have shifted frequently since 1950. Despite certain overlaps and ambiguities, six distinct *tactical* phases of U.S.S.R. policy between 1950 and November 1967 can be identified. This chapter describes the main thrusts of the Soviet position during each of these six tactical phases and suggests some implications for the future.

The First Tactical Phase: Support to Indigenous Communist Party Elements

When NATO was formed in April 1949, Cyprus already was becoming a serious problem for the United Kingdom, which had governed the island as a Crown Colony since 1925. *Enosis* became an increasingly pressing issue during the first years of the 1950s, with spokesmen for the Greek government joining Archbishop Makarios in seeking support for independence and union of Cyprus with Greece. At this time, a hard core of local communist party leaders, many trained in Moscow, was firmly established on the island. Although the Communist Party of Cyprus (AKEL) suffered some loss of influence in the formal political institutions of the island when it failed to win a majority in the May 1949 municipal elections, it nevertheless continued to act as a strong, legalized minority party in a two-party system and gained strength and popular support during the first half of the 1950s. It played a major role provoking unrest and encouraging strikes, ostensibly joining with the opposition Nationalist Party to press for *enosis*. Its activities were enthusiastically endorsed and blatantly encouraged by Moscow.

After the Cypriot Communist Party was outlawed on December 14, 1955, it went underground and commenced a covert campaign for national self-determination, abandoning its earlier pro-*enosis* position. Coincident with this development, Moscow gave less overt support to the Cypriot communists and, like AKEL, temporarily dropped its earlier endorsement of *enosis*. The official Kremlin line became one of vocal support for the "liberation" of the Cypriots from their "foreign oppressors."[19] The U.S.S.R. leaders continued to support the Cypriot communists, but both AKEL and Moscow were comparatively inactive between 1955 and 1959. AKEL excused itself for not supporting EOKA and General Grivas since EOKA asked them "to keep out."[20] This rationalization did not curry favor with either strict Marxist-Leninists on Cyprus or, quite possibly, with the Kremlin leaders. But there was little Moscow could do except wait for the "revolutionary situation" on Cyprus to ripen once more into a phase the communists could effectively exploit.

Active Soviet support of AKEL was intensified after Grivas's insurgency against the British ended in 1959 and AKEL could again operate legally. AKEL had naturally lost considerable ground during the previous five years, although it still claimed approximately 7,000 members. The Soviet position became one of helping AKEL to regain its strength as an opposition political party, to marshal support for eliminating the British military presence, and to increase its potential for revolutionary activities through infiltration of mass movements and organizations.

Summary: From 1950 until Cyprus won limited independence in August 1960, during the first tactical phase identified, the Kremlin worked closely with the indigenous communist party—overtly when circumstances permitted and covertly and less actively during the five years when AKEL was outlawed. Once AKEL had regained its status as a legal political party, it enjoyed Moscow's vigorous and open support in its efforts to recoup its losses and to strengthen its revolutionary potential, both as a political party and as the controlling element in a number of front organizations on Cyprus.

The Second Tactical Phase: Kremlin Attempts to Combine a Cautious Pro-Makarios Posture with Continued Support for AKEL.

The question of British base rights had been more or less settled by the time independence was granted to Cyprus on August 16, 1960. Under the Zurich-London agreements of 1959, the U.K. was to retain its military presence. It was therefore no longer fruitful for the Kremlin—with the assistance of AKEL—to exploit Cypriot dissensions over this issue on a daily basis. This is not to say that total removal of the British military presence on the island had lost importance for Moscow. But new tactics had to be applied. Ways had to be found to manipulate effectively the situation in Cyprus under the changed circumstances without losing sight of the Kremlin's long-term goals: Total elimination of Cyprus from any identification or integration into NATO, utilization of the Cyprus issue to create discord within NATO, and exploitation of the Cyprus problem to divert the attention of the U.S. and the U.K. from more significant issues affecting the East-West competition.

By October 1960, the Kremlin was beginning to adopt a pro-Makarios posture. Moscow sought an expansion of its sphere of influence and control on the island not only through AKEL's five seats in the Cypriot House of Representatives, but also through overtures to the newly elected President, Archbishop Makarios, and the pro-Makarios Patriotic Front Party.[21] At first the Soviet approaches to Makarios were slow and careful. The Kremlin offered to buy the entire 1960 raisin crop of Cyprus and a large proportion of the island's citrus fruit crop in exchange for Soviet timber and cement. Makarios was equally cautious. He said he did not want to accept Soviet aid, but that he might be forced to trade with the U.S.S.R. if the economic situation deteriorated further. Subsequently, Cyprus did conclude the proposed barter agreement with Moscow and this caused a wave of concern within the U.S. State Department.[22] But, like many other nonaligned leaders who are trying to consolidate their domestic positions and formulate their foreign policies, Makarios was clearly attempting to keep all options open without adopting an immediate and blatant procommunist position.

While the Soviet leaders were waiting for Makarios to accept their offer, they were also counting on the indigenous communists to expand their power, which they had begun to regain despite AKEL's limited success in the 1960 parliamentary elections. The strength of the local communists in trade unions and other important organized groups continued to grow. By August 1961, the *New York Times* was sounding this warning: "There is only one country where [the Soviet Union] may reasonably hope to see communism take over by normal democratic procedures. That country is Cyprus. Since independence, [the communists'] hold has expanded as unemployment increased. . . . Some diplomats calculate that, in a free election, the Communists would gain 35% of the vote today. . . . If one recalls the strategic importance of Cyprus, one sees the ultimate danger to the West."[23]

Moscow soon found that it was difficult to woo Archbishop Makarios and also maintain its amicable relations with AKEL. As soon as the Kremlin endorsed the Archbishop's position on *enosis*, its relations with the local communist party became strained even though these differences were comparatively minor. Nevertheless, at the same time, AKEL gained favor by resisting the Chinese communists' attempts to persuade the Communist Party of Cyprus to adopt a pro-Peking line.

The U.S.S.R. and the government of Cyprus had signed a series of trade agreements by December 1961. Because these transactions depended primarily on barter—something the peasants understood—the image of AKEL in the villages was enhanced, thereby accelerating to some extent the growth of the communist mass movement on the island. Throughout 1962 and 1963, Western leaders remained concerned about the threat of a communist take-over in Cyprus.[24] After the 1963 crisis the communists, presumably with the full backing of Moscow, once more switched tactics and sided with Archbishop Makarios. By late January 1964, there were rumors that the Soviet ambassador to Cyprus, Yermoshin, had offered military assistance to President Makarios if needed.[25] On January 30, *TASS* published an official Soviet statement condemning the London Conference on Cyprus, warning the West not to interfere in the internal affairs of the island, and declaring that it was the responsibility of the U.N. Security Council to "safeguard the independence of Cyprus."

By February 17, Soviet arms were reportedly shipped from Egypt to Archbishop Makarios to help him in his efforts both to deter and to defend against the threat of an invasion from Turkey or, quite independently, to liquidate the local Turkish minority on Cyprus itself.

Meanwhile, in the U.N. debate, Soviet spokesmen took every opportunity to castigate the alleged efforts of the NATO powers to "turn Cyprus into a military bridgehead." This was a repetition of standard U.S.S.R. tactics in recent years: To send arms to assist a new nation struggling to consolidate its power and to defend against its enemies, while simultaneously condemning, in public pronouncements by high-ranking Soviet officials, any *Western* interference in the domestic affairs of an emerging nation. As a reaction to these Soviet moves, President Johnson sent a letter to Premier Khrushchev on March 4 urging the Soviet Union to avoid "aggravation of the situation in the eastern Mediterranean."

During the delicate period from March to mid-April, the Soviet Premier tried to persuade Archbishop Makarios to abandon his endorsement of *enosis*. The prospect of further Soviet military aid was the carrot which Khrushchev dangled before the Archbishop. This shift by the U.S.S.R. to opposing *enosis* was understandable: the Communist Party of Greece (KKE) was outlawed, and the same fate probably awaited AKEL if *enosis* succeeded.

Although Makarios did not shift away from endorsement of *enosis* as fully as the Kremlin would have liked, the U.S.S.R. apparently continued to send arms to the

Archbishop. Soviet delegates to the United Nations abstained when a vote was taken on the sending of a peace-keeping force to Cyprus. It was not in Moscow's interest to have a potentially stabilizing U.N. element retard the developing local "revolutionary situation."

Summary: Soviet tactics during our second phase—August 1960 to June 1964—involved continuing support for AKEL, on the one hand, and initiating cautious overtures to the Makarios government, on the other. Both AKEL and Moscow relied primarily on parliamentary tactics supplemented by Soviet economic assistance to Makarios to enhance the possibilities for achieving their mutually shared, long-term revolutionary goal: seizure of power by AKEL. During this period, the Cyprus question was expanded, in the international political arena, beyond an issue among the guarantors of the Zurich-London agreements. It was referred to the United Nations after Turkey threatened invasion. The U.S. became concerned over growing communist influence on the island. Hence, the U.S.S.R. decision-makers were compelled to deal with additional international political elements in their tactical approaches to the problem. The 1963–64 crisis afforded opportunities to attack the principal Western powers for their interference in what the Kremlin termed "Cypriot domestic affairs," thereby enhancing its position with President Makarios.

The Third Tactical Phase: Kremlin Uncertainty and Equivocation

By June 20, 1964, Moscow had reversed its opposition to the U.N. peace-keeping force for Cyprus and had voted for renewal of the mandate for that force. This shift in Kremlin tactics seems to have been motivated by reaction to a more vigorous U.S. stance on the crisis.

Moscow continued its efforts to keep foreign influence —other than its own—out of Cyprus. In notes to Greece, Turkey, the U.K., the U.S., and France on June 19, 1964, the Soviet government urged all recipient governments to seek a solution to the Cyprus crisis solely through the U.N. and strongly suggested that the U.S.S.R. supported full independence for Cyprus free from any outside intervention. This new Soviet emphasis on the U.N.'s role in the crisis was designed to counter President Johnson's efforts to seek an alternative solution through consultations with the Greek and Turkish prime ministers.

Moscow's position was further complicated when the vehemently anticommunist guerrilla leader, General Grivas, returned to Cyprus early in June. The *Economist* of London reported on July 4, 1964: "[Grivas'] reemergence has been quietly encouraged ... by western diplomatic circles [because] he may be able to check the emotional pro-communist wave of feeling. General Grivas has the deepest misgivings about Archbishop Makarios's flirtation with the communist countries."

Faced with this new dilemma, Moscow's behavior became somewhat more ambiguous, although the U.S.S.R. did not abandon its pro-Makarios position entirely. On July 8, Khrushchev again warned against a Turkish invasion of Cyprus, charging that this could cause a dangerous chain reaction. He also repeated his earlier demands for withdrawal of British troops from Cyprus and an end to all Western intervention in the political affairs of the island.[26]

The Greek government now increased its earlier cautious support for Makarios by offering arms and troops in an unsuccessful attempt to forestall further Kremlin initiatives in the conflict and to separate Archbishop Makarios from potential ties to the U.S.S.R. The Soviet position remained ambivalent throughout August despite an appeal from Makarios for Soviet military aid early in the month after Turkish fighters had bombed and strafed Greek Cypriot positions. Soviet hesitancy to support Makarios may have been due in part to U.S. efforts to achieve a peaceful settlement of the dispute via diplomatic overtures to Turkey. Whatever the case, the U.S.S.R. confined itself to a warning to Turkish Premier Inonu on August 9 to stop the military operations against Cyprus, which it claimed were increasing the danger of war. On the same day, Premier Khrushchev assured the Greek Cypriots of the sympathies of the Soviet people and government to the Archbishop's position in the dispute, which now involved military hostilities. However, Khrushchev added that a cease-fire would be an important contribution to peace.

Soviet equivocation had strengthened the U.S. position. On August 9, the U.S. and Great Britain introduced a resolution in the U.N. Security Council appealing for an end to the Turkish bombardment of Cyprus, a cease-fire, cooperation with the U.N. commander by all concerned, and restraint by all countries from actions that might broaden the hostilities. The U.S.S.R. and Czechoslovakia abstained, but the resolution was unanimously passed.

Soviet opposition to the U.N. resolution foreshadowed the adoption of a more vigorous pro-Makarios policy. On August 15, the Soviet Union announced it was prepared to help Cyprus in the event of a foreign invasion and was ready to "begin negotiations on this matter right now." The following day, in a speech at Frunze, Premier Khrushchev said that the U.S.S.R. could not remain indifferent to the threat of an armed conflict near its southern border. He charged that the Turkish air attacks on Cyprus were part of an "imperialist plot" led by the U.S. and Great Britain. He warned that Turkey could not "drop bombs on Cyprus ...with impunity" and that the "harm inflicted on others may act as a boomerang."[27] A new combination of Soviet tactics toward Cyprus was beginning to be applied.

Summary: During the third tactical phase of Kremlin policy vis-à-vis Cyprus, which lasted from late June to the end of August 1964, intercommunal military hostilities were intense and Turkey threatened to invade the island. The U.S. made clear through its position in the U.N. and through unilateral diplomatic moves that it would support the U.N. peace-keeping force and work for a cease-fire. Greece intensified its support for President Makarios. Khrushchev undoubtedly decided that if he went too far he might risk provoking even more vigorous U.S. countermeasures and reduce rather than increase dissensions among the principal NATO powers. While he was not ready to abandon AKEL or to antagonize Makarios, neither did he want to send Soviet troops to assist the Archbishop. Moscow's tactics during this period were somewhat contradictory and cautious. Khrushchev was, in classical Leninist fashion, "buying time" in anticipation of a high-level Kremlin reassessment of the issue.

The Fourth Tactical Phase: Military Assistance Agreement between Moscow and Makarios

In September 1964, a high-level Greek Cypriot delegation visited the Soviet Union for talks. In addition to considerable increase in mutual trade between the two countries, arrangements were made for somewhat more extensive Soviet military assistance to the Greek Cypriots. Supplies of conventional arms, fighters, torpedo boats, anti-aircraft artillery, radar equipment, and rockets were promised.[28] Soviet spokesmen also expressed their displeasure with the operations of the U.N. peacekeeping force. But, as later events proved, the honeymoon between the Greek Cypriots and Moscow was to be short-lived.

The fourth tactical phase of the U.S.S.R.'s approach to the Cyprus problem involved a shift back to a more direct relationship with President Makarios. Between September 1964 and the end of the year, the Kremlin courted Makarios and his followers through offers of arms and expanded economic assistance. Further, to placate the Archbishop for Moscow's earlier equivocation, official Soviet pronouncements voiced loud opposition to the presence of the U.N. peace-keeping force on Cyprus. During this period, AKEL was virtually ignored and left to solve its own local problems. Diplomatic overtures directed toward the now interested Western powers—the U.S., the U.K., Greece, and Turkey—were virtually nonexistent. Apparently, the Soviet leaders had decided that these new tactics would not provoke a more vigorous U.S. series of countermeasures. The U.S.S.R. was repeating a policy it had applied to other newly emergent nations—fulfillment of its doctrinal commitment to support "national liberation movements" through offers of military and economic assistance to the indigenous charismatic leader. The short duration of this phase of the Kremlin's tactics and the fact that the agreements negotiated were not fully implemented suggests that an element of deception was involved. The ouster of Khrushchev after the agreements were negotiated undoubtedly prompted the new U.S.S.R. regime to modify its tactics as soon as it had an opportunity to consider the Cyprus problem.

The Fifth Tactical Phase:
Toward a Pro-Turkish Stance

In January 1965, N. V. Podgornyi led a Soviet delegation to Turkey. Since the U.S.S.R. shares a common border with Turkey, in recent years it frequently has sought to increase its influence over that nation. Podgornyi tentatively indicated during his visit that another shift in the Soviet position on Cyprus was impending. On January 12, he spoke of the "two communities" on Cyprus as having sovereignty, territorial integrity, and legal rights. This long had been the position of the Turkish minority on the island, supported by Ankara.

Podgornyi's remarks were not lost on the members of a Cypriot communist delegation then in Moscow. Relations between AKEL and the Soviet Union were strained because of Moscow's earlier seemingly unequivocal endorsement of *enosis*. (AKEL feared *enosis* because it would lead to its own proscription.) A new note of dissension had now arisen. One must surmise that vehement arguments over the ostensible new twist in Moscow's position on Cyprus were exchanged during the private talks with AKEL's leaders. But the Kremlin did not back away from its support for the "two communities" concept, and even spoke of the election by all the Cypriots of a federated government.

AKEL did not give up easily. It strongly asserted that a federal solution was "wrong and inapplicable."[29] Makarios and Athens also criticized the new Soviet position.

This particular shift in Soviet tactics was probably due, at least in part, to recognition by the new U.S.S.R.

regime of the fact that "unfettered independence and self-determination" would ultimately mean achievement of *enosis* and the extension of Greece's NATO affiliation to Cyprus. Perhaps the Soviet leaders also believed that through closer ties to Turkey they could more effectively pursue their long-term efforts to split NATO and could also exert some control over Turkey, thereby preventing an invasion of Cyprus—a contingency risking both U.S. and Soviet involvement.

In a February 6 report to the Soviet people on his visit to Turkey, Podgornyi again referred to the "two communities" concept. Having noted that "a period that can be characterized as the beginning of the restoration of Soviet-Turkish good neighbor relations has recently set in," he reiterated what he had told Turkish officials and referred to the "legitimate rights" of both Cypriot communities—Greek and Turkish.[30]

Despite its new pro-Turkish position, the U.S.S.R. apparently did not immediately stop its shipments of arms to Archbishop Makarios, although efforts were made to conceal the fact that shipments continued. Perhaps Moscow's leaders felt, after fighting in Cyprus threatened again in March 1965, that there was a real need to try to prevent a Turkish invasion by other than diplomatic means. Whatever the case, the September 1964 arms aid agreement between the Soviet Union and President Makarios seems to have remained in effect during this period. Further shipments of Soviet surface-to-air missiles were reported in May.[31]

Partly because of this development, the Turkish government invited Soviet Foreign Minister Gromyko for talks (May 17–22) and urged that the Soviet Union stop sending arms to the Cyprus government and oppose *enosis*. At a press conference, Gromyko again spoke of "two communities" and reportedly gave assurances in private that there would be no further arms deliveries.[32]

The joint communiqué issued at the close of the visit was less specific. It merely referred to the fact that both sides agreed that all interested parties should "refrain from any actions tending to aggravate the situation in Cyprus."[33] Vexed by what he interpreted as a continued Soviet pro-Turkish position, Greek Premier George Papandreou canceled his plans to make an official visit to the U.S.S.R. the day after the communiqué was published.[34]

This Greek act of protest did not cause the Soviet Union to back down. Between August 9 and 16 the Turkish Prime Minister, Mr. Urguplu, was in the U.S.S.R. on an official visit. In the joint communiqué following these talks, the U.S.S.R. assured Turkey that its position on the Cyprus question remained the same as expressed in its January and May statements. Mention again was made of the need for all interested parties to "refrain from any actions which could aggravate the situation on the island." Once more, the "two communities" concept was set forth as being the mutually agreed position of the Soviet Union and Turkey.[35]

The reaction of AKEL, noncommunist Greek Cypriots, and mainland Greek officials was again critical. AKEL's Secretary General, Ezekias Papaioannou, said that a "solution based on the existence of two separate national communities is wrong, and we completely disagree with it."[36] According to certain sources on August 23, Papaioannou was planning to lead a secret AKEL delegation to Moscow to discuss the communiqué and its implications, but it is unclear if the trip occurred and, in any case the dissension between AKEL and the Soviet leaders continued.

It is also unclear to what extent the Soviet Union continued to furnish arms to the Greek Cypriots during this period, so the precise relations between Makarios and Moscow cannot be determined. On October 17, 1965, a Cypriot official stated that Cyprus had received $70 million in arms aid from the U.S.S.R., about half of which was a gift. However, the surface-to-air missiles that reportedly had been shipped to Cyprus in May via the United Arab Republic now were said to have been returned to the U.A.R. after the Soviet Union began to emphasize a pro-Turkish position.[37]

Early in November 1965, fighting flared up in the Famagusta area of Cyprus. At the request of Turkey, the U.N. Security Council met to consider the new crisis. Although he refrained from taking a pro-Turkish position, the U.S.S.R. delegate, Federenko, did not revert to a pro-Greek Cypriot position, either. He confined himself to reiterating that "the Cyprus question can and must be solved only by peaceful means, in the light of the principles of equity, without any interference from the outside, whatever form that interference from the outside may take."[38] He also repeated the familiar Soviet call for the withdrawal of all foreign troops from the island and the closing of all British bases and mentioned the "two communities" concept. This pro-Turkish position was maintained when, on December 17, the General Assembly's Political and Security Committee debated a pro-Greek Cypriot resolution calling on all member nations to "respect the sovereignty, unity, independence, and territorial integrity of Cyprus and to refrain from any foreign intervention or interference." During the final vote in the Committee, the Soviet Union—and all the Eastern European communist nations—abstained, even though the Political Committee also had before it a Soviet-sponsored draft resolution condemning any interference in the internal affairs of other states.

This Soviet action stimulated an immediate and extremely sharp reaction from the AKEL leadership. The morning after the vote, a statement on the front page of the Cypriot communist newspaper *Haravghi* deplored the U.S.S.R.'s failure to vote for the U.N. resolution.

Despite this plea, the Soviet Union again abstained the next day when the resolution was put to a vote in the General Assembly. All that AKEL could do was to try to forget the matter and hope that the U.S.S.R. would see fit to modify its position in the future along lines more palatable to AKEL's advocacy of support for the Greek Cypriots on the *enosis* issue.

Presumably with that end in mind, AKEL Secretary General Papaioannou and his deputy, Andreas Fantis, flew to Moscow in January 1966 for talks with CPSU Central Committee members Suslov and Ponomarev. After lengthy discussions, a joint communiqué was issued affirming *inter alia* the Soviet belief "that the Cyprus problem can be solved through peaceful means, and that this necessitates the safeguarding of the rights and interests of the two ethnic communities."[39] This part of the communiqué was apparently calculated to please the Turks rather than the Greek Cypriots, and the AKEL leaders must have felt that the U.S.S.R. was no longer firmly behind Archbishop Makarios' position on the future of Cyprus. Makarios himself, in a subsequent interview with a Greek correspondent, indicated that he shared this impression: "With regard to the Soviet Union, I believe that it does not favor a solution leading to union with Greece."[40]

After the AKEL delegation returned from Moscow, having failed to persuade the Soviet leaders to abandon their support of the "two communities" concept, an attempt was made to draw other communist parties into the debate. The February 1966 issue of the *World Marxist Review* carried an article by Andreas Fantis, assistant secretary general of AKEL, reiterating the Cypriot communist position of opposition to "two communities" and federation. Although he blamed the "imperialists" for "the invented theory of two separate national communities", Fantis's implicit criticism of Moscow's policies was surely not lost on the communists who read the article.

Moscow's position posed a dilemma for AKEL. Its leaders were unwilling—or unable—to switch their own position to conform to that of the Soviet Union. As long as the Cyprus problem remained unresolved, it was to AKEL's interest to maintain its profitable façade of unequivocal support for Archbishop Makarios. However, like the Turkish communists who had to sit helplessly on the sidelines while Moscow wooed their "capitalistic" government, the AKEL leaders could not afford to sever their relations with the U.S.S.R. completely.

AKEL had no choice but to adopt a dualistic and highly contradictory position. This position was reflected in Papaioannou's report to the 11th Party Congress of AKEL at the beginning of March 1966. Having expressed gratitude to the U.S.S.R. for its "great help" in preventing the Turks from invading and conquering Cyprus, including the provision of arms, Papaioannou went on to confirm that AKEL still endorsed a pro-Makarios position. He even spoke critically of certain aspects of Soviet policy concerning Cyprus.[41]

Replying to this rebuke, the leader of the Soviet delegation to the Congress did no more than to reiterate the terms—from the outset highly unsatisfactory to AKEL —of the January 1966 Soviet-AKEL communiqué.

Between early March (the end of the AKEL Party Congress) and December 1966, the Cyprus problem received far less high-level attention from the Soviet leaders than it had during the previous year. Once again, at the U.N. Security Council the Soviet delegate voted to renew the mandate of the U.N. peace-keeping force on the island, but he also referred to the "two communities" concept.

That Soviet policy remained pro-Turkish was dramatically confirmed in December 1966 when Soviet Premier Kosygin led an official delegation to Ankara. This was the first time since the formation of the U.S.S.R. that a Soviet head of government had visited Turkey. When the Turkish leaders complained about recent Czech shipments of arms to Archbishop Makarios, Kosygin sided with Turkey against his ally in condemning this act.[42] Whether Kosygin was sincere in his statements to the Turkish leaders that the Soviet Union was not informed of the shipments in advance cannot be determined on the basis of available evidence.

Perhaps because of the embarrassment caused by the Czech arms shipments, Kosygin, in his pronouncements in Turkey, went out of his way to stress the importance of Turkish-Soviet friendship. For example, at a dinner given in his honor in Ankara by Suleyman Demirel, the prime minister of Turkey, on December 20, Kosygin said:

The statements by Turkish statesmen that a Turkish government has firmly embarked on the road of improving relations with the Soviet Union and has no intention of retreating from this road we noted with satisfaction in our country. I would like to make the following observation: By adhering to such a line, Turkey and the USSR cannot lose anything, but can benefit greatly. . . . I would like to make use of my stay here in Ankara to stress that the Soviet

Government intends to continue to promote a friendly policy toward Turkey.[43]

While Soviet leaders frequently are opportunistic in their statements during visits to foreign countries, Kosygin seemed to abandon all caution and concern for repercussions in Cyprus and elsewhere in such effusive statements as this.

Kosygin's other remarks on the Cyprus issue during his visit to Turkey followed the pattern of the majority of official Soviet pronouncements since January 1965, stressing the "two communities" concept. The carefully worded joint communiqué issued at the end of Kosygin's visit left no doubt that the current Soviet position was still pro-Turkish. Moreover, the final phrases of the portion dealing with Cyprus seemed to be an indirect reference to the Czech arms shipments. The communiqué stated:

> The sides exchanged views on the Cyprus question. The Prime Minister of Turkey set down in detail Turkey's stand on the Cyprus question. In turn, the Chairman of the U.S.S.R. Council of Ministers confirmed the Soviet Union's attitude toward the Cyprus question, *as outlined in Soviet statements and also in the earlier adopted joint Soviet-Turkish communiqué. The sides again declared that it is necessary for all states* and members of the United Nations, in conformity with the Security Council resolution of March 1964, *to refrain from actions liable to aggravate the situation in Cyprus.* (Emphasis supplied.)[44]

In the midst of these new expressions of Soviet-Turkish friendship, Turkish activists allegedly urged that the logical next step be taken: Revival of the 1925 Turkish-Soviet Friendship and Nonaggression Pact.

On Cyprus itself, the furor over the Czech arms aid manifested itself in several ways. U.N. Secretary General U Thant's special representative in Cyprus, Mr.

Carlos Bernardes of Brazil, resigned, reportedly because the Greek Cypriot administration refused to place the Czechoslovak arms under U.N. control. General Grivas and anti-Makarios Greek officers supporting him declared that they would sooner or later seize the imported weapons. The Czech arms controversy and the almost simultaneous reiteration of the U.S.S.R.'s pro-Turkish position also prompted General Grivas to call for the annihilation of AKEL.

The Cypriot government officially protested Premier Kosygin's remarks in Turkey on the Cyprus problem. AKEL was again caught in the middle. It could not afford to endorse Moscow's position, nor could it instigate a complete break.

Developments in Greece also added to the confusion toward the end of 1966. The Greek government fell, and the amount of influence which leftist elements could have wielded in the new government was not immediately discernible. Within a few months, this had become an academic question. On April 21, 1967 parliamentary democracy in Greece disappeared altogether when a military junta seized power. The new regime went further than the elected predecessor governments in suppressing the already outlawed Greek Communist Party. It imprisoned all known procommunist leaders, thereby eliminating their influence in communist front groups. These moves stimulated the Kremlin to initiate yet another tactical phase in its policy toward Cyprus.

Summary: The fifth tactical phase of Soviet maneuvers vis-à-vis the Cyprus problem encompassed the period from January 1965 to late April 1967. It was characterized by:

a) Gradual abandonment of political support for and military assistance to Cypriot President Makarios, and

b) Concerted efforts to establish a rapprochement with Turkey. An obvious corollary to the Kremlin's overtures to the Turkish leaders was a shift from endorsement of *enosis* to advocacy of the "two communities" solution to the Cyprus problem long espoused by the Turkish government. This, in turn, led to increased strains in relationships between Moscow and AKEL. The Communist Party of Cyprus still found it advantageous to continue—at least ostensibly—endorsing Makarios' pro-*enosis* arguments. However, AKEL did not break its ties to the U.S.S.R. completely, although a few rebels within the party did organize an abortive effort to draw AKEL into the Chinese communist sphere of influence. Ultimately, the U.S.S.R. responded to Turkish pressures and not only stopped its own arms shipments to Makarios but even condemned subsequent military assistance from Czechoslovakia. These changes in Soviet tactics not only embarrassed AKEL and antagonized President Makarios but also introduced new strains in Soviet relations with Greece, foreshadowing the total breakdown of Greek-Soviet diplomatic interchange during the next tactical phase of Soviet policy toward Cyprus.

The Sixth Tactical Phase: Vehement Anti-Greek and Western "Non-Interference" Posture

Although Soviet propaganda media were comparatively prompt in their vehement condemnation of the violently anticommunist military junta which seized power in Greece on April 21, 1967, it was not until July 5 that an official Kremlin public pronouncement appeared.

Similar to earlier Soviet propaganda following the coup d'état in Greece, a *TASS* statement setting forth the official Kremlin position implied U.S. collusion in effecting the Greek junta's seizure of power. More importantly, it explicitly charged that the new Greek regime was to be used as the tool of the NATO leaders to overthrow President Makarios and to establish a pro-Western military dictatorship on Cyprus. The statement warned:

It is an open secret that the reactionary circles of Greece, supported by the United States and some other NATO members, have long been working on plans against the independence, sovereignty, and territorial integrity of Cyprus. . . . In order that the young state should develop normally, the cessation of foreign interference in the affairs of Cyprus is [now] a matter of high priority. . . . No one must interfere in the internal affairs of the Republic of Cyprus. . . . Only the Cypriots themselves, both Greeks and Turks, have the right to decide their destinies.[45]

The statement went on to charge that the "imperialists" were plotting to make Cyprus a major NATO base for potential aggression against ". . . the Communist countries, the Arab states and national liberation movements. . . ."

Subsequent commentaries in Soviet media have expanded this theme. AKEL's pronouncements since the coup in Greece have been quite similar to those emanating from Moscow. This mutual dislike for the Greek junta seems to have led to an improvement in relations between the Cypriot communists and their Soviet mentors. As will be recalled, these relations deteriorated seriously during the previous tactical phase of Soviet policy toward Cyprus. But AKEL has gone further than Moscow in asserting that any negotiation efforts of the Greek junta and Turkey could eventually endanger Cypriot independence.

Summary: Since the *TASS* statement of July 5, 1967, the Soviet leaders during the sixth tactical phase have adopted an official stance of watchful waiting, although they undoubtedly have tried to influence the Turkish government through diplomatic channels not to agree to a Cypriot settlement which would indeed threaten the continued legal existence of AKEL and its front groups or, more importantly, help to strengthen NATO's southeastern flank. Now that they have committed themselves to vigorous endorsement of cessation of all "foreign" interference in the internal affairs of the Republic of Cyprus, the Soviet leaders must, to preserve their flexibility of action, make the most of their interim moves through private diplomacy instead of through official public pronouncements.

As of November 1967, the complex chain of events involving a new Turkish invasion threat had not yet reached a point where the U.S.S.R. leaders could effectively decide on a new detailed plan of action.

Clearly, Soviet policy toward Cyprus again is in a state of transition. The current tactical phase which began as a consequence of the April 1967 coup in Greece seems to be primarily a holding operation and may not last very long. But as of December 1967 there were too many uncertainties to project future Soviet policy and tactics vis-à-vis Cyprus with any degree of confidence.

Summary Observations

The twists and turns of Soviet behavior toward Cyprus since 1950 testify that the U.S.S.R.'s leaders have no inhibitions about switching tactics—and sides—whenever it appears to be to their advantage. However, two goals of Moscow's policy have remained remarkably consistent: weakening the cohesion of the southern flank of NATO and eliminating the British bases on Cyprus. The endeavor to achieve these goals under changed international circumstances caused shifts in Soviet tactics. Particularly between early 1965 and April 1967, these shifts may have weakened AKEL's prestige and bargaining position with the Greek Cypriot majority government under Archbishop Makarios.

The Soviet leaders, aware that their tactical maneuvers related to the Cyprus problem affect their political interactions with the United States, seem to want to avoid any "backfire" effects that might serve to strengthen the southern flank of NATO by driving the NATO members involved closer together, or otherwise to alter the East-West political-military balance.

As is the case in other geographic areas where the issues are complex, Moscow prefers to act not with tactical consistency but according to opportunity, thereby reinforcing fundamental and unchanged strategic objectives. Given the diversity of the political entities involved in the Cyprus problem and the Kremlin's special and often changing relations with each of them, the Soviet leaders wish at all costs to retain their flexibility. In their view, maintaining a strong position of influence over the affairs of one troubled island and consistently supporting its indigenous communist party is not worth the sacrifice of concomitant advantages elsewhere.

Whether the Kremlin once more will become fairly deeply involved in the Cyprus problem—by renewing arms aid or even considering so drastic a step as direct intervention—will depend in large part on the tenacity of U.S. diplomacy. Moscow has shown a willingness to become involved to some extent in many areas of unrest in the third world and to exploit a local situation to its own advantage whenever a power vacuum has existed. When the U.S. has exerted direct or indirect counterpressures, Moscow in many instances has backed down.

Since the onset of the November 1967 crisis, both the superpowers have had to reassess their positions on the Cyprus problem. But the leaders of both know that complex multilateral negotiations going beyond those which had occurred by the end of the month would be required before the political status quo of Cyprus could be modified by peaceful means and without violation of international law. Both are also aware that a new outbreak of armed struggle between the Greek and Turkish Cypriot communities could begin at any time, changing the entire context of the situation and perhaps postponing indefinitely any hopes that a rapprochement between Greece and Turkey could be the beginning of a viable peaceful settlement of the problem. Clearly, "revolutionary situations" have begun again to ripen on Cyprus and elsewhere in the Mediterranean area. Whether, in the nuclear age, the Soviet leaders will choose to exploit these situations according to classical Marxist-Leninist doctrine, thereby risking a direct military confrontation with the United States, is a question which cannot be answered a priori. It seems more likely that the U.S.S.R. will continue to proceed with caution, confining itself primarily to propaganda attacks and diplomatic maneuvers and delegating to AKEL the responsibility for any overt moves which may be required to try to ensure that the Cyprus problem continues to serve as a source of conflict between Greece and Turkey, their respective ethnic counterparts on Cyprus itself, and the major powers within the NATO alliance.

Given the increasing risks of direct U.S.-Soviet military involvement in a crisis in the Mediterranean area, because of the enlarged Soviet naval presence there and the accelerated strategic importance of that theater of operations, it is particularly important that Moscow tighten its control over AKEL to the maximum feasible extent.

Before World War II, the United States was hardly involved either historically or geopolitically with the British Crown Colony of Cyprus. Since 1955 American strategic interests in the southern flank of NATO and in the Middle East have intensified concern over Cyprus. The continual rise in popular support for the indigenous communist party and its front groups on the island from approximately 1960 onward has caused additional anxiety for U.S. policy-makers.

From its inception in the mid-1950s, the Cyprus problem has strained relations primarily between Greece and Turkey, and the United States has been unable to take a positive stand in favor of either of these two NATO allies at the expense of the other. As a likely consequence the Soviet Union has been afforded a continuing opportunity to delve into Cypriot affairs with the hope of increasing its influence on the island. Developments on Cyprus in the past decade have therefore been of keen interest to the American government.

Reflecting the inherent political dilemma with military struggles between two of its friends, the United States took a rather passive role in the 1955–59 Greek-supported guerrilla campaign against the British in Cyprus. The Greek-American population pressured its congressmen and senators to make advocacy of Cypriot *enosis* an official part of U.S. foreign policy, but these efforts were never fully successful. The U.S. did express the hope that a peaceful solution of the Cyprus problem would be worked out among her three involved NATO allies, and several resolutions to this effect were passed by Congress.[46] Immediately after independence, U.S. policy toward Cyprus was based on four main goals which mirrored American national interest in the Eastern Mediterranean. First, the Republic of Cyprus should develop political stability and join together with Great Britain, Greece, and Turkey to form a solid bulwark against communism. Second, Cyprus should stress economic development, free democratic institutions, and a pro-West orientation. Third, the U.S. should enjoy unrestricted use of its existing communications facilities on the island. Fourth, the British Sovereign Base Areas should remain inviolate and available to any Western nation for any purpose. In exchange for Cypriot recognition of these goals, the U.S. was prepared to offer extensive economic aid and other benefits. U.S. decision-makers welcomed Cypriot independence as the denouement to a difficult foreign policy issue and optimistically hoped that Cyprus could finally be stricken from the "gazeteer of hot spots." This hope was not fulfilled.

Since the 1963 outbreak of violence on the island, U.S. policy has maintained that the Cyprus situation must "be transformed from a danger to a problem." In the legalistic U.S. view, both communities should adhere to the terms of the Zurich-London agreements. But the first step is to maintain law and order with the help of the United Nations peace-keeping force, so as to allow Greek and Turkish negotiators the opportunity to discuss the matter diplomatically. The United States wishes to aid the three guarantor powers and the leaders of the two indigenous ethnic communities in all efforts toward establishing a permanent political settlement in Cyprus, but it also seeks to avoid an excessive national commitment in any such search for a solution.[47] The former U.S. ambassador to the United Nations, the late Adlai E. Stevenson, stated in 1964 that "the United

States has no position as to the form or the shape of a final settlement of the Cyprus problem . . . [thus] it is not for my government to say what that solution should be."[48] This policy of concerned disengagement has remained essentially unchanged as long as the conflict does not threaten to erupt into a Greco-Turkish war.

The maintenance of peace in the Eastern Mediterranean, a major objective of U.S. foreign policy, can only be realized if Greeks and Turks will face one another across a bargaining table rather than through the sights of a rifle. Thus, U.S. policy toward Cyprus is the support of any solution arrived at through negotiations and acceptable to the principal Western powers involved. To this end, America has relied on quiet diplomacy and full support for the stabilizing role of the United Nations. It is noteworthy that this U.S. policy stance is almost identical to the British position, with the possible exception that U.S. interests in Cyprus are more procedural and tactical than substantive.

Of the three crises which are now festering in and near the Middle East—Kashmir, Arab-Israeli, and Cyprus—Cyprus may be the most difficult and perplexing for the U.S., which hitherto has not openly backed one side over the other in these three disputes. If the U.S. should see fit to alter its policy and take sides in the Cyprus struggle, it would mean choosing to support one of its formal NATO allies against another. It is this dilemma that makes the Cyprus issue unique among the three cases. It is conceivable that, should Turkey try to intervene militarily as it has threatened on a number of occasions, the U.S. might feel compelled to interpose the Sixth Fleet either between two of its allies, or against them both. It is doubtful that the NATO alliance could withstand such a jolt.

American-Cypriot Relations: 1960–63

After independence, the fledgling Republic of Cyprus initially sought good relations with the United States while maintaining a neutral posture between the two superpowers and their principal allies. Cooperative efforts between Cyprus and America have been demonstrated most vividly by an aid program designed to further Cypriot economic development. In December 1960, the United States signed the first economic agreement made by the new government, promising to send 50,000 tons of wheat and barley to help alleviate grain shortages caused by drought.

At that time, Dr. Willard Thorp, former U.S. assistant secretary of state for economic affairs, headed a United Nations economic survey team to study Cypriot development potential. The Thorp Report, completed in April 1961, emphasized that the requisite financial aid would have to come largely from external sources.[49] A month later, the United States signed a technical assistance agreement with Cyprus, designed to fulfill the basic recommendation of the report—the establishment of a development bank.

In January 1962, the United States repeated its earlier grant of surplus wheat and barley to ease the lingering effects of the Cypriot drought. This was followed by a Fulbright Educational Exchange Agreement in which the U.S. government gave $300,000 for a three year program. In June 1962, when the American-Cypriot friendship was flourishing, Archbishop Makarios made a state visit to the United States. During the Cypriot President's visit, Secretary of State Dean Rusk made the following formal remarks at a state dinner held in his honor:

Cyprus has not in any genuine sense been independent since the days of the Greek city state. This is an event of the millennium. . . . Cyprus has become independent, through the perseverance, courage, struggles, ability, and dedication of our guest, and has taken its place among the free nations of the world.

Our guest also reminds us of the meaning and the ambiguity in such words as unaligned, uncommitted, neutral. Unaligned, perhaps, in any military sense, with military blocs. That we understand and appreciate. But neutral, neutral, to the great issues facing mankind in the world in which we live? This has not been the case. Uncommitted to us perhaps, but with the deepest commitments of their own —committed to the indispensable moral and constitutional limits upon the exercise of power, committed to the freedom of other peoples, and tolerance toward them, and committed to a decent world order. These thoughts do not disturb us for they are commitments that we basically share.[50]

Following the Archbishop's deliberations with U.S. leaders, a joint communiqué was issued in which the U.S. government expressed its continued interest in furthering Cypriot economic development, which was viewed as being conducive to the maintenance of political stability, the evolution of a pro-Western orientation, and the establishment of viable free democratic institutions on the island.[51] Two additional economic agreements totaling $640,000 for technical assistance were signed shortly thereafter. One provided for the continuance of work on the development bank and the other arranged to provide U.S. agricultural experts for Cyprus and to start a training program in the United States for selected Cypriots. The U.S., in turn, undoubtedly expected protection for and unmolested use of its military communication facilities on Cyprus.

Later in 1962, Vice-President Johnson visited Cyprus to reaffirm U.S. friendship. He "urged a speed-up in Cyprus's economic development" and expressed American concern over the growing communist influence in the island. Johnson warned Cypriot leaders to take into account the threat presented by a strong indigenous communist movement and urged them to act to deter further growth.[52]

In June 1963, the U.S. government announced a Food for Peace agreement by which the government of Cyprus should purchase more than $2 million worth of wheat, and make payment in local currency. One month later, the U.S. Agency for International Development granted Cyprus a $2.3 million loan to help buy American equipment needed for the economic development program and Peace Corps volunteers were sent to Cyprus to work with local government officials to raise agricultural productivity, conduct a geological survey, and improve rural schools. Total U.S. aid to Cyprus through June 30, 1963 amounted to $20 million, including loans, grants, and shipments under the Food for Peace program. But after the outbreak of open intercommunal conflict later that year, U.S. economic aid declined drastically and at present is nonexistent because of the unstable political conditions in the island.

U.S. Efforts to Achieve an Acceptable Settlement of the 1963–64 Crisis

The United States recognized that tension was growing before strife erupted on Cyprus in December 1963 and expressed its willingness to assist the search for a modus vivendi to establish internal order. It was in the interests of the U.S. that a mechanism be found to prevent further communist influence over the island's affairs and the communists were the only ones seemingly profiting from the frustrations of the Republic's government. There was certainly no advantage to the United States to see Cyprus in political turmoil which could be exploited by leftist elements.

On December 26, 1963, President Johnson sent a joint letter to President Makarios and Vice-President Kuchuk expressing grave anxiety over the intercommunal fighting and promising to support attempts to find a peaceful solution. The United States took an active part in the emergency meetings of the United Nations Security Council the same month, but decided to await the outcome of the London Conference on Cyprus in January 1964 before offering to intervene in the struggle. When the conference failed to overcome its deadlock, Britain asked the U.S. to send troops to Cyprus as part of a NATO peace-keeping force. Attorney General Robert Kennedy happened to be in London and took the opportunity to discuss the British proposal. Although no action was taken to commit American troops, this was a first step in what was to become an extensive exercise for America in "crisis management."[53]

On January 28, in the hope of seeking a peaceful solution, President Johnson sent General Lyman L. Lemnitzer, the NATO commander in Europe, as his personal envoy to Athens and Ankara. In both capitals, General Lemnitzer warned the governments of the consequences to NATO if Greece and Turkey were to go to war over Cyprus. This personal appeal staved off unilateral Turkish intervention until a jointly conceived Anglo-American plan could be proposed to settle conditions on the island.

Under the proposed plan, the United States offered to send 1,200 combat troops to Cyprus and to provide the necessary support troops to maintain a NATO peace-keeping force of 10,000 soldiers on the island. The conditions were that the troops would stay only three months, while a European mediator worked out a truce.[54] It took President Makarios only five days to reply. On February 4, he sent word via his foreign minister that he accepted the plan in principle, but wanted the multinational force linked to the United Nations Security Council. Certain other reservations were also mentioned; these were essentially counteroffers. In short, Makarios smoothly rejected the U.S. plan.

In February, Under Secretary of State George Ball, who was to become the leading figure in America's crisis diplomacy over Cyprus, was sent on an urgent peace-seeking mission to the capitals of the three guarantor powers as the special representative of President Johnson. Subsequently, he went to Nicosia to talk with Cypriot President Makarios. His purpose was to convince Makarios that the U.S. peace-keeping plan was desirable and necessary, but his mission failed and the matter was turned over to the U.N. Security Council for debate. Under the leadership of Secretary General U Thant, a U.N.-sponsored peace force for Cyprus was finally agreed upon on March 4. The United States was not asked to supply troops, but it did voluntarily pledge to help pay for the operation, as well as to furnish troop transport as needed. Later that month, bombs exploded in the American Embassy in Nicosia and U.S. dependents were evacuated temporarily from the island. In the three years that followed, the U.N. peace-keeping force was to do an effective job in preventing a recurrence of open hostilities on Cyprus.

On May 4, 1964, President Johnson sent Senator J. William Fulbright on a mission to convey the United States' continuing concern over the Cyprus crisis. Senator Fulbright visited London, Athens, and Ankara to inform these governments of the "sense of urgency felt in the United States regarding the need for the restoration of order on the island." A major reason for the Fulbright mission was to report to President Johnson the impressions of the Greek and Turkish governments concerning Cyprus. The White House emphasized that Senator Fulbright would not attempt any mediation effort or submit any suggestions on behalf of the United States for a political settlement. Nevertheless, by dispatching the chairman of the prestigious Foreign Relations Committee as his personal representative, President Johnson was able to show high-level American interest to the involved governments while simultaneously enlisting sympathy for his Cyprus policy from one opinion leader in the Senate.

A month later the situation became grave and Turkey once again threatened military action to establish a political beachhead on Cyprus. A hastily prepared letter of June 5, 1964 from President Johnson to Prime Minister Inonu was intended to impress sharply that such a course would not be "consistent with the commitment of your [Inonu's] Government to consult fully in advance with us." But the crux of the letter was the threat that Turkey might not receive NATO help in the event of a Soviet attack if her invasion of Cyprus were carried out. Inonu's considered response stressed Turkey's legal right under the 1959 Treaty of Guarantee to intervene to protect the status quo; this was coupled with a firm reminder that the NATO treaty imposes "the obligation to come forthwith to the assistance of any member victim of an aggression."[55]

Inonu visited Washington later that month, after which he obtained an American concession in the June 23 joint communiqué as to the "present binding effect of existing treaties." The same week Greek Prime Minister George Papandreou also visited President Johnson to hear personally why a war between Greece and Tur-

key would be "fraught with such far reaching consequences."[56] But the meeting did not pacify Papandreou
and later during a press conference he took a swipe at
the validity of the "existing treaties." In short, the
talks bore little fruit for America and did nothing to
solve the problem.

The Johnson letter was taken as a serious intervention
in Turkey's sovereign affairs and caused a critical wors-
ening of relations between the two countries. In part because of this episode, Inonu's government fell from
power in 1965. The Johnson letter may also be one ex-
planation for Turkey's later efforts to seek a rapprochement with the Soviet Union—a development which has
certainly brought a better understanding between these
two traditional enemies. Despite his undiplomatic
methods, the President's direct action in 1964 did temporarily stave off a likely head-on conflict between two
American allies; both sides were thankful that they did
not have to go to war over Cyprus. One obvious lesson
learned from the affair was that the United States realized it would not be able to use the same blunt diplomatic
devices again if Turkey were ever to mobilize for another Cyprus invasion, i.e. merely to restrain the Turks
from their legal right to restore the status quo ante
would in fact be to intervene against them. (When the
conflict again heated up three years later in November
1967, the United States did not alienate the Turks with
any similar thinly veiled threats in order to prevent an
imminent Turkish invasion of Cyprus. See below.)

After the fruitless meeting with the Greek and Turkish prime ministers in Washington, the United States
decided to become involved substantively in an effort to
solve the Cyprus dilemma. In late June 1964, Under
Secretary of State Ball proposed to U.N. Secretary
U Thant that Greek and Turkish delegates meet at the

President's Camp David retreat with the American senior statesman, Dean Acheson, who would serve as a mediator. U Thant did not want the U.N. to sponsor a completely American initiative and, thus, made a counteroffer to hold the proposed meeting in Geneva under the direction of the official U.N. mediator, Sakari Tuomioja of Finland. Acheson was invited and went to Geneva as a consultant, but—in deference possibly to the Russians who were then backing Makarios—not as a superpower representative.

It was not an easy matter to arrange a parley between Greeks and Turks at that time, and the President of the United States was urged by Mr. Ball to do what he could to bring the two sides together at Geneva. In early July 1964, President Johnson sent the Greek prime minister an appeal to send a delegate to Geneva, even though Papandreou was convinced the meeting would produce little as far as Greece was concerned. This letter, though intended by the President to be a gesture toward conciliation, was interpreted by Pandandreou as an "ultimatum" to the effect that America would "stand aside" in the event of a Greek-Turkish war. Since Greece had been reminded earlier by Defense Secretary McNamara that she would undoubtedly lose a two-sided war against Turkey, Papandreou reluctantly agreed to send a representative to Geneva in order to meet with the Turks and Dean Acheson.[57] The Greek Cypriot government of Archbishop Makarios was barred from the negotiations at Geneva.

Acheson apparently played a key role at that time. Reports soon leaked out that an Acheson Plan for the future disposition of Cyprus had been formulated. The proposal was to bring Cypriot *enosis* with Greece, but on the conditions that Turkey receive the off-shore Greek island of Kastellorizon, that Turkish Cypriots who wished to emigrate would be compensated, that those Turks remaining would have secure enclaves on the island, and that Turkey would receive a military base in Cyprus. In Acheson's own words, the "plan" essentially was to give Greece its desired *enosis* but also was to provide for Turkey ". . . a military presence unhampered by the need for tripartite consent at every turn. A sequestered base for ground, air and sea forces not only could be a defense for Cyprus but prevent its being used hostilely against Turkey, could defend the sea approaches to the south Turkish seaports, and be a constant reminder on the island of Turkish presence and interest."[58]

The Turks might have been willing to accept a solution giving the major part of Cyprus to Greece as long as they had a guaranteed presence on the island. But the very idea of any part of Cyprus being occupied by Turkey was anathema to Makarios, and Acheson sensed his mission might soon come to naught. In any case, on August 7 Turkish planes began a three day assault on the northwest part of Cyprus. Working through the United Nations Security Council, the U.S. helped to pass a resolution on August 9 calling on the Turks to stop the bombing and the Cypriots to cease firing. Makarios, unable to enlist any outside support for his campaign, called upon Greek Cypriot forces to end hostilities and the Turks immediately reacted by stopping the bombing. Meanwhile, Acheson was still in Geneva and was convinced by this time that the U.S. should stop efforts at forcing an artificial agreement on the Greeks and Turks. Instead, he felt America should disengage itself from the conflict and realize that the matter should be left to Greece and Turkey to work out. Even though the Acheson Plan was to be rejected by all the parties, the American attempt at mediation played an important part in creating an atmosphere for subsequent meetings between Greek and Turkish leaders. The Cyprus crisis of 1964 was a severe test for U.S. diplomats, but the test was passed when war between Greece and Turkey was averted without having to employ any American troops or financial resources.

U.S. Recognition of the Protracted Nature of the Conflict: 1965–67

The aims of U.S. foreign policy toward Cyprus have remained essentially the same since early 1964. They seek to insure that:

a) The conflict between the indigenous Greek and Turkish communities shall not become the cause of a larger war.

b) The protracted political disorder on the island shall not be paramount in U.S. bilateral relations with either Greece or Turkey.

Continually, the U.S. has been forced to play the "honest broker" in the running dispute between these two allies over Cyprus, but this posture has often resulted in making no friends and two enemies. Each time the U.S. contemplates a positive action toward one of the guarantor allies, it must concomitantly run the risk of alienating the other.

Since both mainland Greece and Turkey are equipped with American armaments, the U.S. must continue to be involved in peace-seeking efforts. This was highlighted in 1964 by the intensive, but ultimately unsuccessful, attempts of Dean Acheson to negotiate at Geneva a viable settlement and was again seen in late 1967 with the efforts of Cyrus Vance. Whatever negative attitudes Greece and Turkey and the two ethnic communities on Cyprus now have toward the United States are probably based, first, on the inability of the U.S. to favor one side over the other and, second, on the unacceptable overtures for a peaceful settlement which the U.S. so far has made.

Makarios has continued to seek support wherever he could hope to find it, apparently sensing that no important developments might ever occur on the initiative of the principal external parties to the dispute. For example, in October 1966, while by-passing Washington, he went on state visits to six Latin American nations (Panama, Uruguay, Chile, Peru, Ecuador, and Colombia), where he hoped to explain the problem from his de facto government's point of view and simultaneously raise the prestige of his small country. In conformity with his nonaligned foreign policy, Makarios stated that he made the trip to project Cyprus further into a de Gaullist-type third world. He contended that support for his national cause by third world powers would be desirable, but thus far had been inadequate.

U.S. relations with Greek Cypriots in particular have been strained for a number of reasons. In the 1965 U.N. General Assembly, the United States voted against a resolution emphasizing respect for the sovereignty of the Greek Cypriot Government and condemning foreign intervention in its affairs. This was construed by Makarios to be an act favoring the Turks, even though the U.S. position was solidly based on the fact that the resolution contravened existing treaties. Also, ships sailing under the Cypriot flag have been observed unloading arms and supplies in North Vietnamese ports. The Cyprus government was warned in 1966 of the legislation passed by Congress which prohibits such activity by countries desirous of receiving U.S. aid. When the Cyprus government continued the trade, the U.S. stopped (in November 1966) the little economic aid that was still going to Cyprus. This sanction was rather ineffective since Cyprus was destined to have U.S. aid end by June 1967 under terms of the 1966 legislation which prohibited economic aid to more than the most needy forty countries in the free world. Consequently, the Cypriot practice of trading with an American enemy goes on with impunity.

The latest difficulty in U.S. relations with the Makarios government resulted after the state visit to Washington of the Turkish President Sunay in April 1967 when President Johnson, in a joint communiqué, came out in favor of the "two community" concept. The mainland Greeks as well as the Greek Cypriots felt this was an unnecessarily pro-Turkish position for a friendly nation to assume.

The Soviet Union, as indicated in Chapter IV, now finds itself in a somewhat similar quandary. By trying to support the Greek Cypriot communists' self-determination goal, while concurrently searching for ways to patch up an age-old feud with the mainland Turks who insist on rights for the Cypriot minority community, the U.S.S.R. leaders have experienced some embarrassment from the political necessity to "sit on the fence."[59] For example, there were anti-Soviet demonstrations in Cyprus in the winter of 1966, and a Russian cultural attaché was declared *personna non grata* in early 1967 for alleged spying against the Cyprus government.

U.S. decision-makers are also aware of the obvious motivations for Soviet interest in the island. Apart from the threat to NATO's unity, the island could become a Soviet base for naval operations in the Mediterranean area should the indigenous communist party eventually gain political control. Soviet naval activity in the Mediterranean has increased greatly over the past several years. The current U.S. ambassador to NATO, Harlan Cleveland, has estimated that Soviet naval power in that theater of operations increased tenfold between 1963 and 1966. He stated recently:

Up to 1963, Soviet subs and other warships were infrequently seen in the Mediterranean. Then four years ago, the Soviets decided to build their Mediterranean presence, which NATO's officers have taken to calling the Soviet "Sixth Fleet" . . . By July [1967] a total of forty-six Soviet ships were operating in the Mediterranean including some of the latest guided missile cruisers and about ten submarines together with numerous support ships. . . . Soviet submarine operating days in the Mediterranean have increased by nearly 2,000 percent since 1963.[60]

The Crisis of 1967

The flare-up of intercommunal fighting in November 1967 was as serious as the 1964 crisis. The U.N. peacekeeping force has generally kept the two communities apart in recent years, but this 4,500-man brigade can do little when Greeks and Turks on the island are determined to have it out. This happened on November 15 at a crossroads area thirty miles south of the capital city, Nicosia.

At that time Greek Cypriot police, worried that the Turks were in the process of establishing another armed enclave, tried to enter the mixed village of Ayios Theodorous. This was the first attempt at inspection in four months, when a similar confrontation was dampened by U.N. troops. If the Turks could have created another enclave in that area, they would control the road from Nicosia to the port city of Limassol. The Makarios government was convinced that a repeat of the situation, which for four years has blocked the road to the northern coastal town of Kyrenia, could not be tolerated in the south. Yet the Turks were equally adamant that their way of life in the village not be disturbed by enemy police. When both sides pushed their stands, the result was an eight-hour gun battle. Again U.N. troops stepped in but not before thirty lives were lost, mostly Turks.[61]

Turkey immediately announced full mobilization in preparation for a possible invasion of Cyprus "to settle the problem once and for all by partition of the island." Simultaneously, Ankara gave the unpopular and perhaps weak Greek junta government a way out of war by sending a diplomatic note containing four stern demands: (1) disbandment of the 20,000 man Greek National Guard and removal from the island of the 12,000 illegal Greek Army "volunteers" and of General Grivas; (2) disengagement in the area where fighting broke out and the right for Turkish Cypriots to form their own government and police forces in their enclaves; (3) compensation to the Turkish Cypriots for loss of life and property; and (4) enlargement of the U.N. peacekeeping force. Turkey threatened to invade the island if the Greeks failed to meet all of these demands.

The Turkish demands provided a glimmer of hope and caused a flurry of third party (U.N., NATO, and American) diplomatic activity. To the involved capitals, President Johnson sent former Deputy Defense Secretary Cyrus Vance as a negotiator; U Thant sent Jose Rolz-Bennett of Guatemala as his special representative, and NATO Secretary General Manlio Brosio of Italy offered his good offices. Everyone had the same goal: prevent a war between Greece and Turkey!

It seems clear, even without knowing Mr. Vance's actual instructions, that the United States was not prepared to deter the Turkish invasion by employing military force—an assumption held by some Greek Cypriots and perhaps some mainland Greeks as well—and that the Greek junta government was probably so informed. The United States was prepared to use as much diplomatic persuasion as possible short of military intervention to head off what appeared to be an inevitable military conflict. However, since it intervened against Turkey diplomatically in the 1964 crisis in rather sharp terms, the U.S. would do nothing further to worsen its relations with the Turkish government in the present crisis. This being the case, the only course available to the Greek government short of war was to accede to the Turkish ultimatum.

Greece quickly removed General Grivas from the island and shortly thereafter appointed a civilian foreign minister, Panyiotis Pipinelis, who was thought to be moderate toward Turkey. The moves, obviously, were designed to placate the Turks and give the Greeks more time to consider alternative proposals to the Turkish demands. Also Greece might have harbored the belief that the intervention of third parties might force Turkey to mitigate its terms. Limited as it initially was, Greece did act in a sufficiently positive manner to prove it did not want to go to war over Cyprus. The Turks were not satisfied, and the threat of an invasion continued for two weeks. Mr. Vance labored indefatigably to effect a settlement which would satisfy Turkish demands. At the same time he was concerned about saving face for the Greek government, which had to adhere to this political reality, even though it was probably in a better position to make any unpopular decisions than a democratically elected government would have been.

Mr. Vance's efforts finally met with success as the Greek government acceded to just about everything Turkey had demanded. Greece undoubtedly realized that she could only lose in any military engagement with Turks both in Cyprus and elsewhere. The big stumbling block continued to be the attitude of Archbishop Makarios. He insisted his country was a sovereign power and resisted a provision in the agreement calling for the dismantling of the Cypriot National Guard, which amounts to the country's army. Makarios along with the other principals involved received an appeal from U.N. Secretary General Thant in early December to accept the settlement and thus end the probability of war. In his appeal, the Secretary General suggested an enlargement of the UNFICYP to oversee the demilitarization of the island. It should be clear, however, that even if war has been avoided in the present situation, the underlying issues and tensions still remain and no one can say that anything resembling a lasting settlement has been reached.

Conclusion

While the U.S. policy-makers appear to be between the proverbial Scylla and Charybdis on the problem of Cyprus, they have been relatively effective in efforts to contain the conflict. Employing "quiet diplomacy," the State Department and the able U.S. ambassador to Cyprus, Taylor G. Belcher, have kept communication channels open to the surrounded Turkish Cypriots and with Dr. Fazil Kuchuk, vice-president of the original government of the Republic. Such a relationship is favorably received by Turkey, and so far has not overly alienated the Makarios government. Through this channel, Ambassador Belcher may have played vital roles in cooling off the tempers of the Greeks and Turks (e.g., this contact may have helped to secure the release in

November 1967 of Turkish Cypriot leader, Raouf Denktash).

A series of political or military incidents, major and minor, in the past four years have thus confronted the representatives of both the United States and the United Nations. The UNFICYP "soldiers without enemies" have dampened most of the indigenous flare-ups and, with the help of skillful diplomacy, have miraculously kept the lid on the seething Cyprus caldron. Still the UNFICYP troops are the peace-keepers, not the peace-makers, and they have remained in Cyprus through eleven successive extensions of their mandate because of the inability of mainland Greek and Turkish negotiators to arrive at a mutual agreement which is also acceptable to Archbishop Makarios. U.N. troops provide the only effective buffer between the two warring communities and the consequences of a withdrawal before a lasting settlement is consummated are too grave to contemplate. But the U.N. operation has continually been in debt for a lack of sufficient voluntary contributions, and this complex financial tangle will persistently challenge Western statecraft.

Since 1963 U.S. diplomacy has met with some success: it helped prevent threatened Turkish invasions, thus deterring a Greco-Turkish war; it managed to keep channels of communication open between Greece and Turkey; and throughout the period there was no increase in tension between the United States and Russia.

Perhaps the best summary of the policy dilemmas for the U.S. and its allies remains that offered by former Secretary of State Dean Acheson in a speech before the Chicago Bar Association on March 24, 1965. He said:

The losers plainly are the NATO nations whose alliance has been gravely weakened, and, especially Greece and Turkey whose confidence both in one another and in the

United States and Great Britain has been strained. The gain-ers are the Archbishop . . . the Russians who have weakened NATO and, perhaps, gained another toehold in the Eastern Mediterranean, and Col. Nasser who has added to the fire under his old enemies, the British. On the whole, the story is not the brightest chapter in the diplomacy of the West.[62]

Clearly the problem of Cyprus has not been solved and will remain with us for some time. Another crisis could flare at any moment. It would appear that the best policy for the United States in the short run would be the continued support of the U.N. force and as U Thant has recommended, its enlargement. The cost of such support would be less than the political and other burdens of dealing with the situation on a unilateral basis. Ultimately, it is the challenge of American pol-icy-makers to seek a solution which will be secure, which will deny an opening in the island to the Soviet Union, and which will also be acceptable to Greece, Turkey, and Makarios.

VI. THE OUTLOOK

The uneasy peace which exists in Cyprus in late 1967 is still a potentially explosive situation. To resolve the unhappy state of affairs, the Greek Cypriots would like to see the establishment of a unitary state based on the democratic idea of majority rule. They insist that the Turkish community would be afforded the same minority rights which other countries with similar ethnic heterogeneity have already instituted—for example, the same kind of protection enjoyed by the Muslims of Western Thrace in Greece. To achieve this long-range objective, Makarios will persistently seek to strengthen his hand by *faits accompli* and legal measures, such as the resolution passed in the U.N. General Assembly in December 1965 calling on all member states to "respect the sovereignty, unity, independence, and territorial integrity of Cyprus and to refrain from any foreign intervention or interference." A new constitution institutionalizing majority rule in Cyprus has probably been drafted by the Makarios government. The removal of the Zurich-London treaty barriers and the next general elections (officially scheduled for August 1965, but now postponed indefinitely by fiat) are, however, obstacles in the path of its implementation.

The government of Turkey argues that the independent Republic of Cyprus was established on the basis of the federated principle, involving two separate political entities with equal rights, and *not* on a majority-minority basis. Its leaders insist that without the safeguards for the Turkish Cypriot community incorporated into the

Zurich-London agreements, the independence of Cyprus "would have been unthinkable and impossible."

The various governments of Greece in the past four years have generally backed Makarios in his demands for the future disposition of Cyprus. The accepted belief has been that after majority rule is formalized in the government, Cyprus will then exercise true self-determination, which will result in an overwhelming vote for *enosis*. But the Archbishop has been known to change his mind on numerous occasions and may do so again if he ever has to exercise the option on joining with Greece or not. Thus, Makarios will continue to be an unknown element in all deliberations over Cyprus and may even be able to resist international political pressure to compromise his rigid position.

Following the military coup in Greece in April 1967, it was rumored that the Greek junta was prepared to restore its friendship with Turkey and to offer concessions that would satisfy Turkish-Cypriot objectives. The junta was reported to be willing to:

a) Allow some part of the island to have a form of *enosis* with Turkey, or

b) Consider some alternative solution, such as permitting Cyprus to remain independent but be reorganized on a cantonal basis. (This would allow a considerable measure of autonomy at the local level but involve some additional shifting of the Turkish minority to selected areas of the island.)[63]

Summit talks were held in Thrace during September 1967 between Greece and Turkey, and hope ran high that a solution to the Cyprus problem finally would be reached. It was believed that the new military junta in Greece could make concessions to Turkey and the Turkish Cypriot minority that no democratically elected Greek government could even propose if it is expected to survive at the polls. But these talks broke down because the Greeks again demanded *enosis*.[64] One must take into account the fact that the military junta is not popular in mainland Greece. Even if it were able to effect a peaceful solution to the conflict, it is somewhat doubtful that such a settlement would remain viable any longer than did the earlier compromise arrangements stipulated in the 1959 Cypriot constitution.[65]

Indeed, there is considerable doubt, despite their avowed support of *enosis*, that the principal Cypriot factions involved—the business community, the civil service, and the communists—really want union with Greece. Cyprus now has the highest per capita income in the Middle East with the exception only of Israel— approximately $700 per year. Many businessmen are understandably fearful of what would happen to the island's economy if instant *enosis* with the much weaker Greek mainland economy were implemented. Furthermore, many of the former EOKA fighters who now hold good jobs in the civil service fear a degradation of their positions if the Cypriot civil service were to be merged with that of the metropole. Finally, the communist party, AKEL, fears that union with Greece would lead to its being outlawed and is also very much opposed to having Cyprus become a part of NATO territory. AKEL publically supports *enosis* to enhance its own political advantage, but is rationalizing on this issue by saying that under *enosis* a neutral position for Cyprus could be worked out.

It has become increasingly evident that the Greek and Turkish Cypriots are unable to reconcile their divergent positions, and might never do so peacefully if left to their own devices. For example, on the question of the current international legality of the Zurich-London agreements, the Turkish Cypriots cling to the *pacta sund servanda* principle, while the Greek Cypriots insist that the tacit *rebus sic stantibus* doctrine now is applicable. Thus, the island's Turkish minority favors the perpetuation of the 1959 constitution, while its Greek majority advocates legal—including constitutional—changes designed to insure its complete control over the future foreign and domestic policies of the Cypriot Republic.

The Greeks and Turks in Cyprus have suffered so much at each other's hands that it may be idealistic to expect them to live together any longer on the island. Perhaps the best solution would be a system of property compensation for any Cypriot who wishes to leave. This alternative could be a more sensible resolution in terms of human and economic costs than any other alternatives proposed heretofore. Some Cypriots have already emigrated to more peaceful places, but many militants on both sides remain. Thus far the chief obstacle to any mass migration of Turkish Cypriots has been Ankara's desire for a Turkish presence on Cyprus.

Although the question of Cyprus intermittently has been referred to international organizations for conciliation and resolution, an acceptable, legal, and lasting solution appears to be a long way off. Any potential settlement has two fundamental requirements. First, it must comprehend the present international politico-military realities as well as the realities of the domestic political situation on Cyprus itself. Second, it must be flexible enough to meet changing conditions. Above all, it must motivate the Cypriot people (Greek and Turks alike) to think less in terms of their own selfish interests and more in terms of the international community of which they are part.

1571–1878 A.D.	Ottoman rule—nearly three centuries.
1878–1960	British rule—82 years. 1878: Turkey leased Cyprus to the British. 1914: Britain annexed Cyprus. 1915: the British government offered to cede Cyprus to Greece; offer declined and lapsed. 1924: Treaty of Lausanne, Turkey recognizes British ownership of Cyprus. 1925: Cyprus declared a British Crown Colony. 1931: Movement for *enosis* led to disturbances; 1882 constitution abrogated. 1955: Armed campaign by EOKA launched and Emergency declared. 1956: Makarios and other priests deported for complicity in EOKA campaign. 1959: Zurich-London agreements signed, providing for Cyprus independence with certain conditions.
1960 August	Republic of Cyprus comes into being.
1960–1962	Neutralist foreign policy declared. East-West economic development plan made and foreign aid given. Tension over implementation of constitution.
1963 November	Makarios proposed 13 Amendments to constitution violating basic treaty provisions; Turkey rejects proposals.

December	Violence between indigenous Greeks and Turks. British troops move in to try and keep peace. Turkey threatens to invade Cyprus.
1964 January	London Conference deadlocked, U.S.-NATO (Lemnitzer) Plan not accepted by Makarios.
February	Cyprus matter is referred to U.N.
March	U.N. force landed and mediator, Sakari Tuomioja, appointed.
April	UNFICYP involved in fighting and are unable to curtail violence. Greece and Turkey are dangerously close to war; U.S. engages in "crisis diplomacy."
May	Senator J. William Fulbright, sent to Cyprus on a presidential fact-finding tour.
June	Turkey mobilizes for invasion of Cyprus. Johnson letter deters action, but causes strain in relations between U.S. and Ankara. Greek and Turkish prime ministers visit Washington.
July	Dean Acheson goes to Geneva as mediator.
August	Turkish planes bomb Cyprus; "Achson Plan" rejected by principal parties. U.N. establishes cease-fire.
September	Efforts to bring two sides together prove fruitless.
1965 January	U.S.S.R. begins *rapprochement* with Turkey with support of "federation" for Cyprus.
April	New U.N. mediator, Galo Plaza Lasso offers plan which denies both *enosis* and partition for Cyprus. Plan appeals to Makarios, rejected by Turkey.

May	Soviets deny sending arms to Makarios; agree with Turkey on independence of island with rights of two communities respected.
December	Makarios government receives favorable resolution in U.N. General Assembly.
1966 March	11th AKEL party Congress held; party shows embarrassment as result of Soviet policy maneuvers. Makarios disillusioned with U.S.S.R.
May	Secret ambassadorial-level talks begin between Greece and Turkey, as island conflict reduces in its intensity.
October	Makarios visits U.A.R. and Latin America to extend Cyprus further into third world alignment.
November	Makarios approves of Greek handling of negotiations with Turkey over Cyprus.
December	Makarios concludes arms deal with Czechoslovakia; Turkey registers violent protest. Grivas-Makarios dispute over control of National Guard reaches new height.
1967 April	Greek military coup in Athens causes a reassessment of policy toward Cyprus.
May	Greek junta expresses desire to restore friendship with Turkey and negotiate over Cyprus. Island "normalized through UNFICYP effort. Economy of Cypriot-Greeks prospers.
September	Greek-Turkish summit talks over Cyprus break down when Greece again demands *enosis* for the island. Joint

communiqué leaves door open for further negotiations.

October

Turkish Cypriot leader, Denktash, captured after illegal entry in Cyprus. Turkey demands release to avert any trouble over incident.

November

Denktash released, but violence breaks out shortly after. Turkey threatens another invasion. President Johnson sends Cyrus Vance to serve as mediator in dispute.

December

Vance obtains Greeks' accession to Turkish demands and war is deterred. Makarios at first does not go along with Turkish ultimatum, but appeal from U Thant brings him in line for future negotiations on issue. Makarios stresses Cyprus is a sovereign nation and will not have any solutions forced on it from outside powers. UNFICYP receives 11th consecutive extension of its mandate to expire in March 1968.

GREECE
General

Population: 8,700,000.

Military service: Army and Air Force, 24 months; Navy, 36 months.

Total armed forces: 158,000.

Defence budget 1967: 6,294 million drachmas ($208,000,-000).

Army

Total strength: 118,000.

11 infantry divisions in 3 corps (4 divisions are kept close to full strength).

1 armoured division with M-47 and M-48 *Patton* tanks.

1 Commando brigade.

(Eight divisions near the northern frontier are assigned to NATO: the rest, which are located in southern Greece and Crete, are under national command but are earmarked for NATO.)

2 battalions of *Honest John* surface-to-surface missiles.

M-24 *Chaffee* light tanks.

105mm, 155mm, and 203mm howitzers.

1 surface-to-air missile battalion with *Hawk*.

Most light arms and vehicles are American.

(About 10,000 men of the Greek Army are currently serving in Cyprus.)

Navy

Total strength: 17,000.

3 submarines.

8 destroyers.

4 destroyer escorts.

13 patrol vessels.

5 troop transports.
14 coastal minesweepers.
6 fast patrol boats.
9 tank landing ships.
6 medium landing ships.
23 other ships.

Air Force
Total strength: 23,000; 250 combat aircraft.
2 interceptor squadrons with F-5A (18 planes to a squadron)
1 day-fighter squadron with F-86D.
2 fighter-bomber squadrons with F-104G.
5 fighter-bomber squadrons with F-84F.
1 photo-reconnaissance squadron with RF-84F.
About 30 C-47 and C-119G transport aircraft.
Bell-47 and H-19 helicopters.
(Seven tactical squadrons and one transport squadron are assigned to the Sixth Allied Tactical Air Force; the remainder are under national command.)
1 surface-to-air missile battalion with *Nike-Ajax* and *Nike-Hercules*.

Para-military forces
Gendarmerie: 23,000.
National Guard (Sunday drills): 50,000.
Trained reserves: 175,000.

TURKEY
General
Population: 32,000,000.
Military service: Army and Air Force, 2 years; Navy, 3 years.
Total armed forces: 480,000.
Defence estimates 1967–68: 3,926 million Turkish lire ($439,-000,000).

Army
Total strength: 390,000.
1 armoured division with M-47 and M-48 tanks.
13 infantry divisions, one of which is mechanized.
3 armoured brigades with M-47 tanks.

3 armoured cavalry regiments.
3 independent infantry brigades.
2 parachute battalions.
M-24 light tanks and M-36 tank destroyers.
Honest John surface-to-surface missiles.
105mm, 155mm, and 203mm howitzers.
Apart from some fortress regiments and territorial defence units, all Turkish Army formations are assigned to NATO.
Trained Army reservists number 500,000.

Navy
Total strength: 37,000.
8 destroyers.
10 submarines.
15 coastal escorts.
12 coastal minesweepers.
6 coastal minelayers.
9 support ships.
14 other ships.
Naval reserves: 70,000.

Air Force
Total strength: 53,000; 450 combat aircraft.
8 interceptor squadrons with F-86D/E/K/ (with up to 20 planes each).
2 fighter-bomber squadrons with F-104G.
10 fighter-bomber squadrons with F-5A and F-100.
3 reconnaissance squadrons with RF-84F and F-84R.
4 transport squadrons (C-47, C-54, and C-130).
2 battalions *Nike* anti-aircraft missiles (6 batteries).
The Turkish Air Force, including the *Nike* batteries, is NATO-assigned.

Para-military forces
Gendarmerie: 63,000.
National Guard: 20,000.

SELECTED READINGS

T. W. Adams, *U.S. Army Area Handbook for Cyprus* (Washington: U.S. Government Printing Office, 1964).

Doros Alastos, *Cyprus Guerrilla: Grivas, Makarios and the British* (London: Heinemann, 1960).

Dudley Barker, *Grivas: Portrait of a Guerrilla* (New York: Harcourt-Brace, 1960).

Lawrence Durrell, *Bitter Lemons* (New York: Dutton, 1957).

Charles Foley, *Legacy of Strife* (Baltimore: Penguin Books, 1964).

Sir George Hill, *The History of Cyprus*, Vols. I–IV (Cambridge: Cambridge University Press, 1952).

Charilaos Lagoudakis, "Cyprus 1954–58" and "Greece 1946–49," in *Challenge and Response in Internal Conflict* Vol. II, Chapters 12 and 17 (Washington: Center for Research in Social Systems, American University, 1967).

Stanley Mayes, *Cyprus and Makarios* (London: Putnam, 1960).

Phillip Newman, *A Short History of Cyprus* (London: Longmans, Green, 1956).

Robert H. Stephens, *Cyprus: A Place of Arms* (New York: Praeger, 1966).

Edward Weintal and Charles Bartlett, *Facing the Brink* (New York: Scribners, 1967) Chapter 2.

Stephen G. Xydis, *Cyprus: Conflict and Conciliation 1954–58* (Columbus: Ohio State University Press, 1967).

NOTES

1. Address to the Chicago Council on Foreign Relations, Chicago, Illinois, September 18, 1964.
2. AKEL is the acronym for Anorthotikon Komma Ergazomenou Lao (Progressive Party of the Working People). The only other legal communist party in the Middle East is in Israel; the Syrian Communist Party enjoys only "quasi-legal" status.
3. EOKA (Ethniki Organosis Kyprion Agoniston—National Organization of Cypriot Fighters) was a secret terrorist network formed by Grivas in 1953 with the stated purpose of fighting "for the liberation of Cyprus from the British yoke." The sanguinary conflict waged by EOKA lasted four years before an armistice was declared upon the promise of independence for Cyprus in 1959. The British were never able to subdue EOKA completely, despite the use of an estimated 30,000 troops. Survivors of the EOKA underground emerged as heroes, and many now hold important posts in the government of Cyprus. Grivas, who has never softened his hatred for the communists, had been in command of the Greek Cypriot National Guard, composed partly of "volunteers" from the regular army of mainland Greece, until November 1967.
4. C. Foley, ed., *The Memoirs of General Grivas* (New York: Praeger, 1965), p. 35.
5. *Haravghi* (Nicosia), December 8, 1960.
6. Quoted by AKEL Deputy Secretary-General Andreas Fantis in *Neos Dimokratis* (Nicosia), June 1960.
7. The revised AKEL program was set forth at the party's 10th Congress in March 1962, and was published as *The Program of AKEL* by Printko, Ltd., Nicosia (Kaimakli), 1962.
8. U.S. Department of Labor, Bureau of International Labor Affairs, *Directory of Labor Organizations* (Europe), (Washington, D.C.: U.S. Government Printing Office, May 15, 1965), Vol. I, pp. 5.1 and 5.10.
9. *Pravda* (Moscow), March 3, 1966.
10. Andreas Fantis, "The Rise of Socialism," *Neos Dimokratis*, April 1961.
11. *Haravghi*, June 5, 1960.
12. *Ibid.*, September 29, 1963.

13. Speech delivered by Secretary-General Papaioannou at the AKEL 11th Congress, March 3, 1966, carried by *TASS International Service Broadcast*, March 3, 1966.

14. Personal interview with Ziartides, August 1965. The Acheson Plan of September 1964 proposed that, in exchange for *enosis*, a military base on Cyprus would be ceded to Turkey along with a small Greek island and the Turkish community would be given two cantons under its own administration (See Chapter V).

15. *The Cyprus Mail*, August 29, 1965.

16. *Haravghi*, June 5, 1960. Interestingly enough, the possession of five seats in the fifty-member House does not, according to the constitution, make AKEL a recognized political party in that body. Article 73, par. 12 of the constitution reads: "Any political party which is represented at least by 12 percent of the total number of Representatives in the House of Representatives can form and shall be entitled to be recognized as a political party group."

17. *The Program of AKEL*, 1962.

18. Papaioannou was re-elected Secretary General of AKEL at a plenary meeting of the central committee held in conjunction with the 11th Party Congress, March 1966.

19. Statement by N. S. Khrushchev, *TASS*, May 4, 1958.

20. "Democritus" (Pseudonym of George Cacoyannis), *The Leadership of AKEL and the Armed Struggle* (Limassol, Cyprus, privately published, May 1959). This passage was quoted in the Introductory Note, p. ii, which was signed simply "S"—which may be assumed to be the code name of Ploutis Servas, former AKEL Secretary General and long time critic of the present leadership of the Cypriot communists.

21. Ironically, this party was formed by former members of EOKA. Apparently, AKEL had learned from its setback during its opposition to EOKA's insurgency against the British that it would have to increase its flexibility if it ever was to regain its former significant influence in key Cypriot political institutions. Whether this coalition arrangement was made at the urging of Moscow is a question which cannot be answered on the basis of available data.

22. *The Economist*, November 19, 1960.

23. *New York Times*, August 12, 1961.

24. *Christian Science Monitor*, September 28, 1963.

25. *Die Welt*, January 29, 1964.

26. *Pravda*, July 4, 1964.

27. *Pravda*, August 17, 1964.

28. *The Times*, London, October 7, 1964.

29. *Haravghi,* January 26, 1965.
30. *Pravda,* February 7, 1965.
31. *Washington Post,* May 7, 1965.
32. *London Observer,* May 23, 1965.
33. *Pravda,* May 23, 1965.
34. *New York Times,* May 25, 1965.
35. *Pravda,* August 17, 1965.
36. *Haravghi,* August 19, 1965.
37. *The Times,* London, October 25, 1965.
38. *United Nations, Security Council, S/PV. 1252,* November 5, 1955.
39. *Pravda,* January 25, 1966.
40. *Kathimerini* (Athens), March 9, 1966.
41. *AKEL News Letter,* November 1, 1966, pp. 23; 44.
42. Attempts apparently were made by Makarios and the Czech government to keep their arms agreement secret, and personnel loyal to the Archbishop were entrusted with unloading the Czech arms upon their arrival on Cyprus. As late as December 5, a Greek Cypriot spokesman denied any knowledge of an arms deal. But on December 6 reports from Athens said that a fourth shipment of 150 tons of arms, including heavy machine guns, armored cars and bazookas already had arrived on Cyprus. The reports added that another shipment was expected soon.
43. *TASS International Service Broadcast,* December 20, 1966.
44. *TASS International Service Broadcast,* December 27, 1966. Earlier, during the pro-Makarios phase of Soviet policy, the U.S.S.R. leaders at the U.N. and elsewhere had expressed some reservations about the 1964 Security Council resolution.
45. *Pravda,* July 5, 1967.
46. See for example: U.S. Congress, House, *H. Res. 172* and *H. Res. 173,* 86th Cong. 1st Sess. February 16, 1959; also *Congressional Record* (Senate) Vol. 105, *ibid.* (The House sponsors were Reps. Dent and Libonati, both of Italian descent.)
47. T. W. Adams and Alvin J. Cottrell, "The Cyprus Crisis," *Orbis.* Vol. III, No. 1, Spring 1964, *passim.*
48. United States Mission to the United Nations, Press Release No. 4417, June 19, 1964.
49. Willard L. Thorp, *Cyprus—Suggestions for a Development Programme,* ST/TAO/CYP/1 (New York: United Nations, 1961).
50. U.S. Department of State. Press Release, June 6, 1962.
51. U.S. Department of State *Bulletin,* June 25, 1962, p. 1011.
52. *New York Times,* August 31, 1962. It was reported then that Cyprus was entertaining a "fifty-man Soviet Embassy, three times the size of the American Embassy staff."

53. For a more detailed look at the behind-the-scenes activity on Washington's highest level at this time see John C. Ausland and Col. Hugh F. Richardson, "Crisis Management: Berlin, Cyprus and Laos," *Foreign Affairs*, Vol. 44, No. 2, January 1966. Cf. Edward Weintal and Charles Bartlett, *Facing the Brink* (N.Y.: Scribners, 1967), Chapter 2, "Aux armes, Citoyens!" George Ball was supposed to have used the French phrase in an appeal to Acheson to keep pressure on both the Greeks and the Turks in August 1964.

54. The "Lemnitzer Plan" is feared by leftist elements, since they feel it may be "revived" by the West. The plan is described by the leftists as: "staged intercommunal friction, Turkish intervention, pseudowar, elimination of the Cyprus state, bilateral talks, and partition." See Dr. Vassos Lyssarides, "Cyprus and the Middle East Crisis," *Review of International Affairs* (Belgrade), Vol. XVIII, August 5–20, 1967, p. 8.

55. See the exchange of correspondence in *The Middle East Journal*, Vol. 20, No. 3, Summer 1966, pp. 386–93.

56. The military aspects of a possible Greco-Turkish war are considered at length in T. W. Adams, "Crisis in Cyprus," *Army Magazine*, Vol. 15, No. 2, September 1964, pp. 26–34.

57. Weintal and Bartlett, *Facing the Brink*, p. 30.

58. Address to the Chicago Bar Association, March 24, 1965. The phrase "double *enosis*" was also used to describe the Acheson proposal.

59. "Russia's Good Neighbour Policy On Show," *The Interpreter* (London), September 1965, pp. 5–8.

60. Address to the National Press Club, August 23, 1967.

61. The prelude to this incident was the arrest of the expatriated Turkish Cypriot leader, Raouf Denktash, who had landed illegally in Cyprus on October 31. The continued detention of Denktash was a *cause célèbre* for both the mainland and island Turks, as well as a potential excuse for another serious outbreak of violence. Ankara denied involvement with the "Rudolph Hess-type" escapade, but nevertheless demanded of Greece and Makarios that Denktash be sent back to Turkey. After ten days of legal maneuvering, Denktash was released, much to the dismay of Greek extremists headed by General Grivas. The Ankara government probably felt that their pressure on the Greeks had been effective, and it was not surprising to see them push this advantage to the hilt with the subsequent four demands after violence had broken a long period of calm in the island.

62. Address to the Chicago Bar Association, March 24, 1965.

63. This alternative was first formally suggested by Dean Acheson in 1964.

64. According to one dispatch, these bilateral talks at Kesan in Turkey and Alexandroupolis in Greece almost broke down until the Greek Army "strongman," Col. George Papadopoulos, personally intervened. Papadopoulos reportedly advised his colleagues not to press the *enosis* issue and to allow the talks to continue so both sides could exchange suggestions. While these summit meetings did not produce the long-awaited settlement, a friendly joint communiqué was issued which stated that both sides "agreed to continue through the appropriate ways, the exploration of possibilities to bring closer their views on the Cyprus issue," *Washington Post*, September 11, 1967.

65. A detailed study of the Cypriot constitution and the problems that it generated may be found in T. W. Adams, "The First Republic of Cyprus—A Review of an Unworkable Constitution," *The Western Political Quarterly*, Vol. XIX, No. 3, September, 1966, pp. 475–90.

STUDIES IN INTERNATIONAL AFFAIRS

These studies, three to six of which will be published
each year, reflect the Center's major continuing interests:
the examination of trends in international politics and
the assessment of America's evolving foreign policy. They
will analyze and comment on issues of current interest
to policy makers, the academic community, and informed
persons generally.

New in the series:

5. ALLIANCES AND THE THIRD WORLD
   By George Liska $1.75

6. FIFTY YEARS OF SOVIET FOREIGN
   POLICY
   By Herbert S. Dinerstein $1.95

7. CYPRUS BETWEEN EAST AND WEST
   By Thomas W. Adams and Alvin J. Cottrell $2.25

Published in 1967:

1. INTERVENTION AGAINST
   COMMUNISM
   By Herbert S. Dinerstein $1.45

2. IMPERIAL AMERICA
   By George Liska $2.25

3. CRISIS OVER RHODESIA
   A Skeptical View
   By Charles Burton Marshall $1.45

4. THE CHANGING STATUS OF GERMAN
   REUNIFICATION IN WESTERN
   DIPLOMACY, 1955-1966
   By Charles R. Planck $1.45

THE JOHNS HOPKINS PRESS, Baltimore, Maryland

In and of itself Cyprus is economically and militarily an insignificant factor in world affairs. Yet, as events have demonstrated—in the Congo, Vietnam, and elsewhere— the ongoing rivalry between East and West virtually assures that any conflict, however minor, contains the potential for escalation. In large measure, the crisis in Cyprus is a result of these international conditions. The Soviet Union has tried to exploit the Cypriot unrest in an effort to gain influence in the area and to disrupt the Western alliance, while the United States has had to walk a diplomatic tightrope so as not to strain its relations with Greece and Turkey, members of the NATO Alliance. In this authoritative study, the authors describe and analyze the historical roots of the Cyprus problem, the extent of local communist influence, Soviet policy toward Cyprus, the crisis of 1967, and U.S. policy toward the conflict and its ramifications. Their lucid examination of the issues involved is essential reading for students, policy makers, and informed citizens.

THE JOHNS HOPKINS PRESS, Baltimore, Maryland 21218